D0895349

DISCARDED

978.7
L 334w

978.7   L334W C.1
LARSON, TAFT ALFRED

WYOMING   Norton,

                                 the Nation

978.7 L334W WYO

CX007125531

1. Wyomi   II. Series.

THE STATES AND THE NATION SERIES, of which this volume is a part, is designed to assist the American people in a serious look at the ideals they have espoused and the experiences they have undergone in the history of the nation. The content of every volume represents the scholarship, experience, and opinions of its author. The costs of writing and editing were met mainly by grants from the National Endowment for the Humanities, a federal agency. The project was administered by the American Association for State and Local History, a nonprofit learned society, working with an Editorial Board of distinguished editors, authors, and historians, whose names are listed below.

EDITORIAL ADVISORY BOARD

James Morton Smith, General Editor
Director, State Historical Society
of Wisconsin

William T. Alderson, Director
American Association for
State and Local History

Roscoe C. Born
Vice-Editor
The National Observer

Vernon Carstensen
Professor of History
University of Washington

Michael Kammen, Professor of
American History and Culture
Cornell University

Louis L. Tucker
President (1972–1974)
American Association for
State and Local History

Joan Paterson Kerr
Consulting Editor
American Heritage

Richard M. Ketchum
Editor and Author
Dorset, Vermont

A. Russell Mortensen
Assistant Director
National Park Service

Lawrence W. Towner
Director and Librarian
The Newberry Library

Richmond D. Williams
President (1974–1976)
American Association for
State and Local History

MANAGING EDITOR

Gerald George
American Association for
State and Local History

Wyoming

A Bicentennial History

T. A. Larson

W. W. Norton & Company, Inc.
New York

American Association for State and Local History
Nashville

Copyright © 1977
American Association for State and Local History
All rights reserved

Published and distributed by W. W. Norton & Company, Inc.
500 Fifth Avenue
New York, New York 10036
Printed in the United States of America

Library of Congress Cataloguing-in-Publication Data

Larson, Taft Alfred, 1910–
  Wyoming: a Bicentennial history.

  (The States and the Nation series)
  Bibliography: p. 187
  Includes index.
  1. Wyoming—History. I. Title. II. Series.
F761.L32 1977   978.7   77–3592
ISBN 0–393–05626–0

978.7
L334w

1 2 3 4 5 6 7 8 9 0

pub
8.95
7–77

Contents

Illustrations

CX0071265001

YUMA CITY-COUNTY LIBRARY
Yuma, Arizona

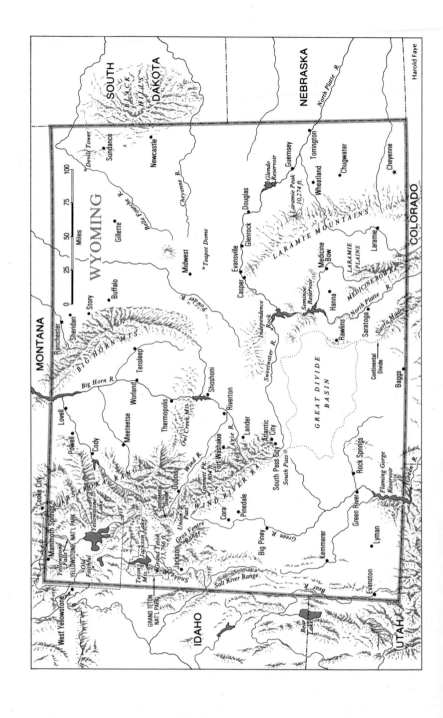

WYOMING

Harold Faye

Invitation to the Reader

IN 1807, former President John Adams argued that a complete history of the American Revolution could not be written until the history of change in each state was known, because the principles of the Revolution were as various as the states that went through it. Two hundred years after the Declaration of Independence, the American nation has spread over a continent and beyond. The states have grown in number from thirteen to fifty. And democratic principles have been interpreted differently in every one of them.

We therefore invite you to consider that the history of your state may have more to do with the bicentennial review of the American Revolution than does the story of Bunker Hill or Valley Forge. The Revolution has continued as Americans extended liberty and democracy over a vast territory. John Adams was right: the states are part of that story, and the story is incomplete without an account of their diversity.

The Declaration of Independence stressed life, liberty, and the pursuit of happiness; accordingly, it shattered the notion of holding new territories in the subordinate status of colonies. The Northwest Ordinance of 1787 set forth a procedure for new states to enter the Union on an equal footing with the old. The Federal Constitution shortly confirmed this novel means of building a nation out of equal states. The step-by-step process through which territories have achieved self-government and national representation is among the most important of the Founding Fathers' legacies.

The method of state-making reconciled the ancient conflict between liberty and empire, resulting in what Thomas Jefferson called an empire for liberty. The system has worked and remains unaltered, despite enormous changes that have taken place in the nation. The country's extent and variety now surpass anything the patriots of '76 could likely have imagined. The United States has changed from an agrarian republic into a highly industrial and urban democracy, from a fledgling nation into a major world power. As Oliver Wendell Holmes remarked in 1920, the creators of the nation could not have seen completely how it and its constitution and its states would develop. Any meaningful review in the bicentennial era must consider what the country has become, as well as what it was.

The new nation of equal states took as its motto *E Pluribus Unum*—"out of many, one." But just as many peoples have become Americans without complete loss of ethnic and cultural identities, so have the states retained differences of character. Some have been superficial, expressed in stereotyped images— big, boastful Texas, "sophisticated" New York, "hillbilly" Arkansas. Other differences have been more real, sometimes instructively, sometimes amusingly; democracy has embraced Huey Long's Louisiana, bilingual New Mexico, unicameral Nebraska, and a Texas that once taxed fortunetellers and spawned politicians called "Woodpecker Republicans" and "Skunk Democrats." Some differences have been profound, as when South Carolina secessionists led other states out of the Union in opposition to abolitionists in Massachusetts and Ohio. The result was a bitter Civil War.

The Revolution's first shots may have sounded in Lexington and Concord; but fights over what democracy should mean and who should have independence have erupted from Pennsylvania's Gettysburg to the "Bleeding Kansas" of John Brown, from the Alamo in Texas to the Indian battles at Montana's Little Bighorn. Utah Mormons have known the strain of isolation; Hawaiians at Pearl Harbor, the terror of attack; Georgians during Sherman's march, the sadness of defeat and devastation. Each state's experience differs instructively; each adds understanding to the whole.

The purpose of this series of books is to make that kind of understanding accessible, in a way that will last in value far beyond the bicentennial fireworks. The series offers a volume on every state, plus the District of Columbia—fifty-one, in all.

Each book contains, besides the text, a view of the state through eyes other than the author's—a "photographer's essay," in which a skilled photographer presents his own personal perceptions of the state's contemporary flavor.

We have asked authors not for comprehensive chronicles, nor for research monographs or new data for scholars. Bibliographies and footnotes are minimal. We have asked each author for a summing up—interpretive, sensitive, thoughtful, individual, even personal—of what seems significant about his or her state's history. What distinguishes it? What has mattered about it, to its own people and to the rest of the nation? What has it come to now?

To interpret the states in all their variety, we have sought a variety of backgrounds in authors themselves and have encouraged variety in the approaches they take. They have in common only these things: historical knowledge, writing skill, and strong personal feelings about a particular state. Each has wide latitude for the use of the short space. And if each succeeds, it will be by offering you, in your capacity as a *citizen* of a state *and* of a nation, stimulating insights to test against your own.

James Morton Smith
General Editor

Wyoming

Introduction

"Powder River!" men cry, a wild surge in their throats.
For this is the land of the few against the unpersonal
much; Of uncommunicative spaces and stoic horizons, and
the consciousness of holding on; . . .

—W.O. Clough, 1949

*U*NTIL very recently Wyoming has been a have-not state
with a very small population. Its location, resource limitations,
high elevation, and aridity have combined to impede growth.
The country simply could not sustain many people.

Sparsity of population has been characteristic of the area
since primitive times. The first known human beings in the area
were paleo-Indian hunters and gatherers who may have come on
foot from Siberia by way of Alaska 20,000 years ago or more.
University of Wyoming anthropologists led by Prof. George C.
Frison in 1975 excavated a site near Worland where some of
these ancient hunters killed and butchered six immature ice-age
mammoths 11,200 years ago. The site yielded projectile points,
knives, bone tools, and stacked piles of bones. Other Frison
teams in the 1970s excavated several bison traps where ancient
men butchered herds of *Bison antiquus* at a slightly later time
than that of the butchered mammoths. The *Bison antiquus* was
larger than the *Bison bison* of modern times, which is popularly
known as buffalo. The ancient hunters drove the bison into ar-
royo traps to their death or into deep sand, as at a Casper site,
where they floundered until they could be killed.

Other excavations have uncovered evidence that early people
were present in what is now Wyoming, but probably the perma-

3

nent population was low. Many Folsom sites (which take their name from the town of Folsom, New Mexico, near which an important discovery was made in 1925) have been located and some of them excavated. Later than the 10,500-year-old Folsom culture is the Mummy Cave site, thirty miles west of Cody, in which a 1,300-year-old mummy was found in one of the upper levels. Many levels have been studied in this cave where people lived continuously for thousands of years, beginning about 9,000 years ago. In eastern Wyoming primitive men quarried quartzite which they used to make projectile points and a variety of chipped stone tools. Hundreds of pits, some of them twenty feet wide and almost that deep, are scattered over an area extending forty miles north to south and ten miles east to west in Niobrara, Goshen, and Platte counties. Many tons of reject material remain. Probably the workers who did the quarrying came from considerable distances over a period of millenia, and stayed only long enough to obtain their raw material. They preferred to live in other areas, and like many people since, took what they came for and left. (In the 1870s cowboys who discovered the pits thought that the Spaniards had been there digging gold, and named them the Spanish Diggings. Many scientists from the East visited the area in the 1880s and 1890s. They dismissed the Spanish-origin theory and carted off to eastern museums most of the artifacts worth preserving, leaving some in a museum in Douglas, Wyoming.)

About 7,000 years ago the region seems to have become arid, causing game animals, and the people who depended on them, to leave the Wyoming country, or seek refuge at high elevations. A few people remained in the mountains, in Mummy Cave, for example, but otherwise the region was largely depopulated for 2,000 years or more, judging by the failure of anthropologists to find much evidence of human life.

Then, about 4,500 years ago people began to come back to the Wyoming country with improving climate and returning animals. For the next 2,000 years quite a number of so-called Middle Period sites have been found. With further improvement in the environment more people turned up, many modern artifacts appeared, and the Late Period began about A.D. 500.

Not much is known about the natives of the area before A.D. 1800. From what *is* known, however, it can be said with some confidence that the Wyoming country supported fewer people than that of surrounding areas. There were probably no more than 10,000 nomadic Indians in Wyoming when the white men came. Buffaloes, the mainstay of these hunters, did not thrive in Wyoming as greatly as they did to the east. But besides the lack of food, the population was kept down by intertribal wars.

From about the eighteenth century on, several tribes competed for the best hunting grounds. The Shoshonis occupied most of Wyoming. The Crows lived in the Big Horns and on the plains to the east. Beginning in the eighteenth century, the Arapahos and Cheyennes, who had migrated from the northeast, warred on the Crows and Shoshonis. Then in the early nineteenth century the Oglala and Brulé Sioux moved out of South Dakota, joining the Cheyennes and Arapahos in driving the Crows into the Big Horns and the Shoshonis to the area west of the Continental Divide.

From the number of governments claiming ownership one might get the impression that the area was highly prized. Spain, France, Great Britain, Mexico, and Texas all claimed parts of the Wyoming country at various times. In fact, however, the many claims meant only that Wyoming lay at the upper ends of river systems and on the Continental Divide. Claims staked out at the mouths of rivers covered the drainage basins unless other claims intervened. Although Wyoming has been figuratively under six flags, only one, the Stars and Stripes, has literally flown over it.

Wyoming is in 1976, as it was in 1776, too high, dry, and cold for the needs and tastes of most people. Also, much of the soil is rocky, sandy, shallow, alkaline, or otherwise unsatisfactory. The Indians did not disturb the soil, nor have the white men plowed more than 7 or 8 percent of it. One reason is the altitude: with an average elevation of 6,700 feet, Wyoming is higher than any other state except Colorado. Wyoming's most famous newspaper editor, Bill Nye, a century ago wryly observed that "during the winter it does not snow much, we being above snow line, but in the summer the snow clouds rise above us, and thus the surprised and indignant agriculturist is caught in the middle of a July day with a terrific fall of snow, so he is virtually compelled to wear his snowshoes all through his haying season." [1]

Despite the harshness of climate and landscape, Wyoming's mountains and plains offer a pleasing prospect to the eye. "Across the plain we could see the mountains," wrote Ernest Hemingway of Wyoming,

> They were blue that day, and the snow on the high mountains shone like glass. The summer was ending, but the new snow had not yet come to stay on the high mountains; there was only the old sun-melted snow and the ice, and from a long way away it shone very brightly. [2]

It is hard to find a point in the state from which it is impossible to see mountains because there are several small ranges scattered across the country in addition to the larger ranges—Big Horn, Medicine Bow, Wind River, Absaroka, Gros Ventre, Owl Creek, and Uinta. From the middle of the southern border the Continental Divide extends to Yellowstone Park in the northwest corner; en route it follows the crest of the Sierra Madres, the rim of the Great Divide Basin, and the crest of the Wind River Range.

Surprisingly, the mountains are not as high as those in Colorado: Gannett Peak, the highest, reaches to 13,804 in the Wind Rivers, and the Grand Teton is only 13,766. And, in fact, most of Wyoming, while high in altitude, is not mountainous—from the High Plains in the east, across the intermontane basins to the Rockies, the land is mostly treeless except for willows, cottonwoods, and brush along the streams and evergreens on the mountain slopes. Bunchgrass, shortgrass, and sagebrush dominate the range on the plains.

Perhaps one reason that Wyoming did not develop large centers of commerce is the fact that its rivers are all small and

1. Bill Nye, *Forty Liars and Other Lies* (Chicago: Donohue, Henneberry & Co., 1890), p. 203.

2. Ernest Hemingway, "Wine of Wyoming," in *The Short Stories of Ernest Hemingway* (New York: Charles Scribner's Sons, 1927–1953), p. 462.

are known only as tributaries of larger streams: the Snake begins in the Tetons but waters Idaho, mostly, before flowing into the Columbia; the Green has carved a spectacular canyon in the southwestern corner but spends most of its journey in Utah on the way to the Colorado River; and the smaller rivers in the north end up in the Missouri, which receives three times as much water as the Columbia and Colorado combined.

The lack of water, more than anything else, seems to have placed a lid on population growth. In this semiarid land, the average annual precipitation is only about 14.5 inches. A dozen mountain ranges get more than the average, and the Red Desert in the southwest and the northern part of the Big Horn Basin get no more than six inches (anything below ten inches a year is considered desert). A high evaporation rate (forty-eight inches per year) and pre-emption of water rights by downstream states make matters worse for development-minded residents. Scatter the state's 375,000 people over its almost 100,000 square miles and you have only one small family for each square mile of land. It is this small population, from earliest times to the present, that has set Wyoming apart from other states and given its people both advantages and disadvantages.

Wyoming—why, and why not? Why did most people choose to go through it or remain in it for only a short time, and then go away? Why did a few hardy souls take on what most people saw as only a windswept plain or life-defying mountain wilderness? And why did Wyoming develop the way it did? Or to put it another way, why did *not* Wyoming develop? Because compared to other states, the story of Wyoming has to do more with nondevelopment than steady upbuilding. Nevertheless, there is a story, one of hardihood and heroism in a state that became the home of the fur trade rendezvous, a state that was the first to grant equal rights to women. It is a story, too, of rascality and romance as the emigrants made their way west over the trails and as cattlemen began to work their ranches. The concluding chapter of the story will certainly involve the less personal matter of energy development; but as we will see, the people of Wyoming are concerned that in the sweep of development the human values that have made Wyoming not be lost.

1

The Fur Trade Territory

*Not a hole or corner in the vast wilderness of the
"Far West" but has been ransacked by these hardy
men . . . and these alone are the hardy pioneers
who have paved the way for the settlement of the
western country.*

—*F. Ruxton, 1847*

*T*HERE were not many mountain men—they probably
numbered only in the hundreds even at their zenith. Their era
was short, roughly from 1820 to the 1840s; and their contribution was limited. They did not intend to "make history" but
only to live in freedom and make money trapping for pelts. But
they played a unique role in opening up the mountain West to
the Americans. The knowledge they gained of geography,
weather, game, and plantlife was passed on to the emigrants
who came West and to those who settled there. Not everything
the mountain men did added to human life: they were vicious in
their methods of fighting, and although they lived like Indians
and many took Indian wives, they had no hesitation in killing
Indians when it served their purposes.

Perhaps more importantly, the mountain men established an
image of the free-roaming individual who lived in the wilderness, unhampered by the restraints of civilization. The image

sometimes outran the reality—the mountain men were out to make money, after all, and they depended on civilized society for many of their needs, including guns and liquor. Nevertheless, more than the cowboy, the pioneer-settler, or any other frontiersman, the mountain men achieved an independence from civilization. Here he is as depicted by one writer:

> The mountain man was almost Indian-colored from exposure to the weather. His hair hung upon his shoulders. He was bearded. Next to his skin he wore a red flannel loincloth. His outer clothes were of buckskin, fringed at all the seams. The jacket sometimes reached to the knee over tight, wrinkled leggings. His feet were covered by moccasins made of deer or buffalo leather. Around his waist was a leather belt into which he thrust his flintlock pistols, his knife for skinning or scalping, and his shingling hatchet. Over one shoulder hung his bullet pouch, and over the other his powder horn. To their baldrics were attached his bullet mould, ball screw, wiper and an awl for working leather. When he moved he shimmered with fringe and rang and clacked with accoutrements of metal and wood. The most important of these were his traps, of which he carried five or six, and his firearm with its slender separate crutch of hardwood
> . . . . Peering vividly out from under his low-crowned hat of rough wool, he was an American original as hard as the hardest thing that could happen to him.[1]

A good thing, too, that the mountain man had a tough skin, not only for the grizzly with which he might tangle in the forest, but also for the nights of frozen, below-zero bitterness and for the hard bite of arrow and tomahawk. The mountain men also must have had the proverbial cast-iron insides, since according to one contemporary their favorite meat was cougar, shading only slightly dog flesh in the canons of mountain cuisine. Because wilderness life assured irregular mealtimes, when food presented itself the mountain men ate with "real gusto" anything they could find—which meant buffalo hump and beavertail when you could get it, and insects, horse blood, and the leather thongs of moccasins when other fare was absent. The manners and morals of these "American originals" matched the

1. Paul Horgan, *Great River: The Rio Grande in North American History* (New York: Holt, Rinehart and Winston, 1954; 1971 edition), p. 464.

sensitivity of their palates. Fur trappers spoke a peculiar, coarse language, apparently influenced by the high nasal tones of Indian talk, although no one cared (or dared) to report literally, the earthiness of their language. Their individualism sometimes led to a sort of "every man for himself" tactic when under fire. The mountain men also shared with Indians a predilection for scalping enemy dead.

Although the fur trade never amounted to much in the total economy of the United States, it was nearly the entire economy of Wyoming for many years. And all the white actors on the Wyoming stage before 1840, with very few exceptions, were connected with the fur trade. An account of some of these men and their experiences shows why few people chose to live in the harsh land of Wyoming.

It seems likely that the first fur traders to visit the Wyoming country were two French Canadians, the brothers François and Louis Joseph Vérendrye. They came from Canada by way of the Mandan villages in North Dakota in 1742–1743, probably touched the northeast corner of what is now Wyoming, and possibly reached the Big Horn Mountains. The explorers' father, Pierre Gaultier Varennes, Sieur de la Vérendrye, had promised the French Government in 1731 that if he could have some fur trade monopolies on the Canadian frontier around Lake of the Woods and Lake Winnipeg, he would look for a shortcut to the Western Sea at his own expense. One misfortune after another caused him to postpone the promised search. Finally, in 1742 the pressure from Versailles, via Quebec, became so insistent that Vérendrye, who was ill and impoverished, sent the two sons.

François was 27; Louis Joseph was 25. They were experienced frontiersmen, having trapped and traded under their father's supervision for several years. One of the two was known as the Chevalier, which one cannot be established with certainty. The Chevalier had accompanied his father to the Mandan Indians in 1738–1739. The Vérendrye brothers, accompanied by two French servants, left Fort La Reine in Manitoba April 29, 1742, and arrived at the Mandan villages (probably at the present site of Mandan, North Dakota) on May 19. There they let most of the summer slip away, while they waited for the

"Horse" Indians to come in to trade. They hoped that the Horse Indians would let them travel west with them on their way home. Concluding, finally, that the Horse Indians were not coming, the Vérendryes left the Mandan villages on July 23 with their two servants and two Mandan guides.

For the rest of the summer and well into the fall the Vérendryes moved slowly southwest, staying with the "Handsome Men" Indians, then the "Little Foxes," both friendly tribes. Finally they reached the long-sought Horse Indians in October and found out that none of them had ever been to the Pacific Coast; that they were, in fact, deathly afraid of the Snake Indians. The brothers then moved on to the Belle Riviere tribe and then the Bows. The Vérendryes proceeded to join an abortive attack the Bows and their allies launched against the Snakes. On January 1, 1743, the Bows and their party sighted high mountains and began to move toward them through "magnificent prairies" full of "wild animals." But the war party dispersed after discovering an abandoned Snake camp. The Vérendryes then started home, burying an inscribed lead plate on a bluff overlooking the Missouri River. (School children found the plate 170 years later, in 1913, at Pierre, South Dakota.) The Journal they kept disappointed the minister of marine in Versailles so much that the Vérendryes lost their fur trade monopolies.[2]

The Vérendryes represent the contribution of the French to the fur trade that eventually developed. Moving along the rivers, the French became adept at cultivating Indians, who supplied them with pelts. The French, more than the British and many Americans, seemed to appreciate Indian ways and adopted Indian customs, took Indian wives, and learned Indian languages. But the Vérendryes themselves were not interested in Wyoming and indeed were afraid of what they might find

---

2. The best available copies of the Vérendrye Journal in existence today appear to be the identical ones in longhand preserved in the Bibliothèque Nationale, Paris, and the National Archives of Canada, Ottawa. Printed texts in French and English are published in Lawrence J. Burpee, *Journals and Letters of Pierre Gaultier de Varennes, De La Vérendrye and his Sons,* trans. W. D. LeSueur (Toronto: The Champlain Society, 1927). Other, less reliable, translations in English are published in *South Dakota Historical Collections* 7 (1914): 349–358, and *Oregon Historical Quarterly* 26 (1925): 116–129.

there. They were seeking a route to the Western Sea, and Wyoming lay in the way. They never returned to Wyoming, nor did any other white man before the nineteenth century, so far as we know.

The next intervention of whites into Wyoming country resulted, in part, from international politics. After the Louisiana Purchase in 1803, Lewis and Clark began their expedition but did not pass through what is now Wyoming—they missed it by sixty miles. However, they came in contact with another principal in the Wyoming fur trade story: François Antoine Larocque.

Lewis and Clark came across Larocque at the Mandan villages in the winter of 1804–1805, where several French Canadians and a Canadian Scot were representing the British North West Company. Larocque, the leader of the Canadian traders, sought to learn what they might expect from the new owners of Louisiana. However, the Americans, particularly Lewis, resented the Canadians and refused Larocque's request for permission to join their expedition.

In the spring of 1805, two months after the Americans had headed northwest toward Montana, Larocque, under orders from his company, headed southwest toward the Big Horn Mountains of Wyoming, accompanied by two servants and a large company of Arikara, Crow, and Snake Indians (mostly Arikara) who were returning to the Rockies after a trading session at the Mandan villages. They rode up the Powder River and Clear Creek, reached the site of present Buffalo in August, and then turned northwest to the Big Horn and Yellowstone rivers before returning to Canada.

Larocque told the Indians at the outset that he had been sent by "the chief of the white population to smoke the pipe of peace and friendship . . . and to accompany them as far as their country and to explore it and take account of whether there were beavers there as had been related, in order to induce them to hunt." [3] Larocque had three packhorses loaded with trade

3. The Larocque Journal in English may be found in John Hakola, ed., *Frontier Omnibus* (Missoula: University of Montana, 1962), no. 1, pp. 1–28; and also in Paul C. Phillips, ed. *Historical Reprints from The Frontier* (Missoula: University of Montana, 1934), no. 20, pp. 1–26.

goods that he distributed generously along the way. Most of the goods went for beaver skins. The servants, Souci and Morrison, showed the Indians how to prepare the pelts. Larocque's eagerness to promote the harvest of beaver led him to disregard the usual inhibitions about taking pelts in summer. At the end of his tour he reported that he had bought 122 beaver pelts "not in consideration of what they were worth (because they are all summer skins) but in order to show to the savages the value that I attach to the beaver skins and to the goods that we give them." With his superiors in mind he added that "at the same time I wished to be able to prove that there are beaver in this region. . . ."

Larocque learned that while beaver dams adorned the whole length of the Powder River, it might take some time to convince the Indians of the value of the beaver trade. He wrote in a classic understatement that some of the natives "seemed to desire that I go away." The Indians hinted that the twenty-three pelts Larocque had taken up to that time were "a great many more than we needed." The Indians, like whites who were to come and endure fur trapping for only a short time, disliked trapping beaver for money.

The Larocque Journal includes other information that probably interested his employers: the fact that the Snake Indians placed great value on blue beads, that the Powder River was always muddy and "scarcely drinkable," that August nights could get very cold along the Powder, and that many buffalo, deer, antelope, and bear lived in the area, although the land between the Powder and the Little Missouri was remarkably dry and had "scarcely any vegetation."

Larocque did in fact go away and stay away, though not for the Indians' reasons. When he said farewell to his hosts on September 14, he asked them to "kill beaver and bear during the whole winter" because he would return the following autumn with all the trade goods they desired. However, the North West Company decided to concentrate on expanding in Canada for the time being, and Larocque never came back to Wyoming.

But absence of the French Canadians was more than compensated for by the succeeding rash of white Americans who entered Wyoming to trap and to explore. John Colter became the first white American to reveal the wonders of Wyoming geography, although there remains some doubt about where he went and what he saw. Colter was with the Lewis and Clark expedition as it returned in 1806 and encountered two trappers in present-day North Dakota who persuaded Colter to go trapping with them. Since they could use Colter's knowledge of the Montana country, the trappers offered to outfit him if he would enter a partnership with them. Lewis and Clark detached Colter at the Mandan villages after exacting promises from all the other members of the expedition that they would not ask for the same privilege.

Presumably Colter and his partners trapped in the Crow country of northern Wyoming. They did not prosper; perhaps they quarreled. In the spring of 1807 Colter paddled a canoe down the Missouri all by himself until he met a fur trade party of forty-two men led by Manuel Lisa, prominent Spanish fur trader out of Saint Louis, at the mouth of the Platte. For the second time Colter postponed his return to Saint Louis. Lisa's party included three other veterans of Lewis and Clark's expedition— George Drouillard, John Potts, and Peter Wiser—who probably had a hand in arranging for Colter's employment by Lisa.

The Lisa party arrived in October at the confluence of the Big Horn and Yellowstone rivers, where some of the men built a trading post and others trapped, and where John Colter received a special assignment to search for Crow Indians in northwestern Wyoming and invite them to the new trading post. Presumably he found one village and learned there about others. He carried a thirty-pound pack loaded with items with which he could win good will and hire guide service. When Lisa gave Colter this assignment he unwittingly marked him for future fame, for in conducting the search he discovered what came to be called Colter's Hell, Jackson Hole and Yellowstone Park.

The official Journals of Lewis and Clark, published in 1814, included a map of their route with a dotted line added to show where Colter went. On this map the topography around Colter's route is peculiar in several respects, which should not be surprising, considering that Colter made a 500-mile hike in the dead of winter, kept no notes, had never done any mapping, conveyed his information to William Clark from memory three years later, and died before he had a chance to check the map. However, the map bears too much resemblance to modern maps of the area to be dismissed as imaginary. Particularly significant is the presence of two large lakes corresponding to Jackson and Yellowstone lakes and a large river flowing north out of one, as the Yellowstone River does.

The thermal activity observed by Colter, to which the name "Colter's Hell" was later applied, was on the Shoshone River just west of present Cody, Wyoming. Little thermal activity occurs there now, but there is evidence to indicate that there could have been a good deal of it in Colter's time. Colter might have seen hot springs and geysers at West Thumb but he missed by at least twenty miles the major geyser basins of what became Yellowstone Park.

The National Park Service Museum at Moose in Jackson Hole exhibits a rhyolite lava stone, thirteen inches long, on which is carved "John Colter" and "1808." An Idaho farmer plowed up this stone in 1931 just west of Jackson Hole. There is no way to establish the authenticity of the stone.

Almost as well known as his discovery of the Yellowstone Park area is Colter's footrace later in 1808 northwest of Yellowstone Park. Captured by Blackfeet Indians, Colter was given an opportunity to run for his life. Stripped naked and hotly pursued, he ran six miles to a stream where he concealed himself in driftwood until nightfall when very quietly he stole away. Seven days later he arrived at Lisa's fort with sore feet and a sunburned back.

After other narrow escapes Colter returned to Missouri in 1810, got married, and settled down on a farm. Probably the mountains would have lured him back sooner or later, had he not died of yellow jaundice in 1813. In 1976 the splendid Colter Bay tourist facilities on Jackson Lake made an impressive memorial for this heroic discoverer of the area. His fame all over the country has made many people think of remote, sparsely settled Wyoming, something that practically no one was doing in Colter's own time.

For some years few people believed the Colter stories about the wonders of northwestern Wyoming. Then the Blackfeet Indians and a German-born, New York-based fur trader unwittingly combined forces to send many more whites through Wyoming in one year than had been there in all previous years. John Jacob Astor, head of the American Fur Company and its subsidiary, the Pacific Fur Company, sent Wilson Price Hunt overland in 1811 to take charge of a trading post which a seaborne party was building at Astoria, Oregon, at the mouth of the Columbia. Hunt's expedition, known as the Overland Astorians, was the first expedition to cross the continent after Lewis and Clark. Astor's original plan called for Hunt to follow the route of Lewis and Clark, but fear of the Blackfeet in Montana caused him to leave the Missouri River at the Arikara villages at the present line of the South Dakota–North Dakota border and head toward the Big Horn Mountains of Wyoming. Three Lisa veterans—John Hoback, Jacob Reznor, and Edward Robinson—who had recently come in across northern Wyoming and had joined Hunt's party, recommended the change of plan. Perhaps John Colter, who had talked to Hunt in Missouri, also suggested that the Blackfeet should be avoided.

After trading their boats for horses at the Arikara villages, the Astorians began their overland journey in July 1811. Many of them had to walk because most of the horses were loaded with packs of merchandise for the trading post at Astoria. As it extended along the Grand River in northern South Dakota, the caravan included sixty-two men, one woman, and two children. The party must have crawled slowly from day to day as it wended up the rivers and across the grassy plains, a landscape stirred by occasional dust devils in the summertime and broken up only occasionally by landmarks like Devils Tower, the rocky volcanic core that can be seen for twenty miles across the plains. Making and breaking camp with such a multitude must have been an enormous undertaking, but not entirely unpleasant in the early stages when the party was well-stocked with supplies. Then there would have been rich moments around the campfire, since two-thirds of the men were French Canadians, who, Washington Irving said, were "ever ready to come to a halt . . . make a fire, put on the great pot, and smoke, and gossip, and sing by the hour." [4] The Astorians moved up the Little Missouri and across the dry hot corner of what is now northeastern Wyoming, up the Little Missouri until the Big Horns loomed blue in the distance, streaked with snow, throwing their bulk in the way of the travelers.

The redoubtable Edward Rose served as a guide until he left to join his people, the Crow Indians, in the Big Horns. Rose, who was one-half white, one-fourth Cherokee, and one-fourth black, had been adopted by the Crows a few years earlier when he had been trapping and trading in northern Wyoming as an employee of Manuel Lisa.

A member of the expedition had warned Hunt that Rose intended to desert when he reached Crow country, would take other men with him, and would make off with some of the horses and packs. Taking this warning seriously, Hunt had made it a point to treat Rose with special generosity. When Rose chose to ask for release, Hunt paid him half a year's salary, and instead of losing horses, he was able to replenish his herd by purchase (with some of his trade goods) from the Crows. Not only was the parting friendly, but a few days later when the Astorians found themselves stymied by the mountain barrier, Rose returned with some Crows to show the way through the southern Big Horns to the Wind River.

So the Astorians passed over the Wind River Mountains through Union Pass and down into the Green River Valley by mid-September. At that time of the year the nights are typically cool, even cold, and the sky a brilliant canopy of stars, the Milky Way gleaming like a silver carpet overhead. The yellow cottonwoods and golden aspen, brought on by the declining sunlight, throw the black-green slopes of forest into relief. And the Wind River ridges and peaks themselves, the highest in Wyoming and still today among the most remote in the country, rise up in stone majesty, territory fit only for grizzlies, timber wolves, and eagles. Camped by a stream of chill snow runoff, hearing perhaps the splashing of an elk herd crossing in the

4. Washington Irving, *Astoria* (New York: Putnam's, 1868), p. 183.

twilight, the air pungent with pine and spruce, the Astorians had their treasure in the experience and we can only wonder if they appreciated the wonder of it all.

Hunt explored down the Green a short distance, observing as he went that it appeared to be "very favorable for hunting beaver." He found fearful Shoshonis who had never seen white men before. After winning their confidence he traded with them for a dozen beaver pelts and noted that they seemed pleased when he promised to return for further trade. Hunt would never return, but many other representatives of his company would. This was a momentous meeting for both the American Fur Company and the Shoshonis, hinting at many years of trade and fights and parleys.

Advancing into Jackson Hole posed no problem since Hunt had three guides who had been there before. Hunt named the Hoback River after one of them. When they left Jackson Hole via Teton Pass in early October, the Astorians could contemplate their Wyoming experience with satisfaction. They had learned much about northern Wyoming while enjoying a generally pleasant trip, free from Indian hostility and serious privation. They had seen Wyoming's high country in August and September when it is at its best. The ordeal that lay ahead of them is another story. They finally staggered into Astoria in February 1812.

Astoria accidentally forged another link in the chain of Wyoming history. Problems at Astoria induced Wilson Price Hunt and his associates to send a seven-man party overland to John Jacob Astor in New York. A 27-year-old Scot, Robert Stuart, who had gone to Oregon by ship, led the party which left Astoria June 29, 1812. Like Hunt, Stuart was a minority partner in Astor's Pacific Fur Company.

The eastbound Astorians entered Wyoming in September 1812 along Bear River on what would later be known as the Oregon Trail.[5] Six of the seven members of the party had traveled west with Hunt the year before; so they were familiar with one cross-

5. Philip Ashton Rollins, ed., *The Discovery of the Oregon Trail* (New York: Charles Scribner's Sons, 1935), pp. 163–167 and Notes.

country route. But a Shoshoni in Idaho had told them about South Pass and had recommended it as superior to Union Pass in crossing the Continental Divide. Unfortunately their plan to go directly to South Pass misfired because of an argument with twenty-one overbearing Crow Indians on Bear River. One gigantic brave insisted on having Stuart's horse until he was driven away at pistol point. Trying to avoid further trouble from the Crows, the Astorians detoured to the north and got lost. They were on Grey's River in Star Valley when, early one morning, the Crows stole all their horses.

The Astorians decided that they must obtain other horses. In a search for friendly Shoshonis they floated down the Snake River into Idaho on rafts, after burning everything they could not carry. They wanted to leave nothing for the Crows. Unable to find the Shoshonis, they walked back through Jackson Hole and over the rim to the upper Green River Valley. They had been without food for a week when a French Canadian in the party proposed that lots be cast, with Stuart excused, to determine who should accept cannibalism. With cocked rifle in hand, Stuart rejected the suggestion. The next day they shot a decrepit buffalo bull, large portions of which they devoured in a "ravenous manner."

A few days later they met some Shoshonis who had recently lost all their horses to the Crows except for one nag which Stuart procured in exchange for a pistol, an axe, and a knife. Using the horse to carry their gear, they climbed the gradual incline to South Pass with new spirit. The summit of the pass is only 800 feet above the point in Green River Valley where they began their ascent. Anxious to avoid a Crow village located, according to the Shoshonis, on a river on the east side of the pass, they crossed the Continental Divide, not on a well-worn Indian trail, but well to the south of it. Thus their passage from the western slope to the eastern occurred either at the southern edge of the twenty-mile-wide South Pass, or, more likely, just south of the pass. Although they discovered South Pass, the Astorians may not have gone *through* it.

Once over the Continental Divide, the Astorians meandered slowly eastward, finally taking the Sweetwater to the North Platte, not reaching Saint Louis until April 30, 1813, when the

Missouri Gazette reported: "By information received from these gentlemen, it appears that a journey across the continent of N. America, might be performed with a waggon, there being no obstruction in the whole route that any person would dare to call a mountain in addition to its being the most direct and short one to go from this place to the mouth of the Columbia River. . . ."

Thus the returning Astorians were the first white men to travel along much of what would become known as the Oregon Trail. They suffered more in Wyoming than the Wilson Price Hunt party because of the starving time in Jackson Hole in October, and because they were too few to protect themselves against hostile Indians.

Like all white men who had come into Wyoming up to this time, the returning Astorians were connected with the fur trade. Like Hunt's westbound party, they reported to the American Fur Company the presence of beaver, at least in a few places. Larocque, Colter, and the two Astorian expeditions acquired much information about Wyoming and made the place better known, but they offered no encouragement for people to make the place their home. The two Astorian parties thought of Wyoming mainly as a barrier, though rather easily overcome, between John Jacob Astor's eastern and far western trading enterprises.

In the next decade Wyoming remained on the outer fringes of the fur trade, whose centers were Montreal, Saint Louis, Taos, and Fort Vancouver (British North West Fur Company) on the Columbia. In 1820, probably a thousand or more employees of the fur trade could be found on the Missouri River and its tributaries, while fewer than fifty were in the Wyoming country. Missouri Fur Company men entered from the Yellowstone, some of them going all the way south to the North Platte where they met Spanish traders from New Mexico. Among the pioneers in the southeast, Jacques LaRamie has received much more attention than anyone else, although he continues to be a shadowy figure whom no one has been able to pin down definitely. According to a popular story he was a free trapper whom Arapahos killed somewhere on the Laramie River in 1820. So smoothly does his name roll over the tongue that pioneers loved it and applied it to rivers, mountains, a peak, some plains, a county, a city, and a chapter of the DAR.

Donald Mackenzie of the British North West Company brought a brigade into the Green River Valley from the west in 1820–1821. This the British were entitled to do during the years 1818–1846 when Great Britain and the United States jointly held the Oregon Country. Mackenzie returned to the Green in 1823 as a Hudson's Bay Company leader after it had merged with the North West Company in 1821.

The Wyoming fur trade quickly expanded to its maximum potential in the 1820s. Unlike the Missouri River trade in which Indians did most of the trapping, the Wyoming trade depended mainly on white trappers. The dominant trader and employer of trappers at the outset was Gen. William H. Ashley. He visited Wyoming only twice, in 1825 and 1826, but quite a few of his employees later rose to prominence on their own. General Ashley's small advertisement in a Saint Louis newspaper in February 1822, inviting 100 "Enterprising Young Men" to ascend the Missouri River and work for him and his partner, Andrew Henry, is certainly the most famous advertisement in fur trade history.

The men who reached the Rockies as a consequence of answering Ashley's advertisement became known first as mountaineers, and later as mountain men. Indeed, Ashley is sometimes credited with introducing into Wyoming's Green River Valley a unique breed of free, fearless, independent men.

Ashley (1778–1838) was a forceful, aggressive, fearless Virginian, perhaps five feet, nine inches tall, and weighing about 140 pounds. In 1803 he moved to Missouri where he worked in lead mining, trading, surveying, real estate speculation, and the manufacture of gunpowder. In his business dealings he showed ruthless ambition. He served as a captain of militia in the War of 1812; after he was elected lieutenant governor of Missouri in 1820 he obtained promotion to brigadier general. He failed to be elected governor in two campaigns, but served in the U.S. House of Representatives, 1831–1837, where he won recognition as an expert on the West.

The first Ashley-Henry partnership suffered terrible reverses at the outset. A Missouri River snag cost them a keelboat and its

$10,000 cargo in 1822. Then on June 2, 1823, the Arikaras killed fourteen and wounded forty-seven of their men. Higher up the Missouri, the Blackfeet killed other Ashley-Henry men. The powerful opposition of these two tribes caused the partners to move their operations to the central Rocky Mountains. To get there, they left the Missouri River in present South Dakota and went overland, as Wilson Price Hunt had done. Major Henry went up the Grand River with about thirty men in late August 1823, and continued on to the upper Yellowstone River. In late September, Jedediah Smith led a second Ashley-Henry party of about fifteen men up the White River and around the south side of the Black Hills before advancing through the Big Horn Mountains. Wyoming chambers of commerce, always eager for population growth, should honor the Blackfeet and the Arikaras for changing the minds of Hunt's Astorians and Ashley's mountaineers and steering them toward Wyoming.

Grizzlies slowed both Ashley parties on their way to the mountains in 1823. Hugh Glass absorbed such a mauling on the Grand River that no one thought he could survive. Major Henry waited several days for him to die, then decided to leave two men, Jim Bridger, 19, and an older man named Fitzgerald, to care for him during his last hours, while the others pressed on to the Yellowstone. Several days later, Bridger and Fitzgerald overtook their fellows, reporting that poor Glass had expired. A month later, Glass turned up at Fort Kiowa on the Missouri River. Perhaps he owed his life to the flow of adrenalin resulting from his towering rage at being deserted. Bridger and Fitzgerald had left him with only a knife. He had crawled and staggered 100 miles to Fort Kiowa, muttering maledictions all the way. It was not an auspicious beginning for the neophyte Bridger, but the stain on his escutcheon would fade in later years as his laudable deeds multiplied.

Just about the time Hugh Glass stumbled into Fort Kiowa, it was Jed Smith's turn to grapple with a grizzly sixty miles south of where Gillette, Wyoming, is now. Jim Clyman sewed one ear back in place and repaired several other wounds as directed by the barely conscious Smith. The whole party waited ten days or so for Smith, who was not as close to death as Glass had been.

Sooner or later, every mountain man tangled with a grizzly bear or with a black bear that became a grizzly after the story had been told a few times. Most of the time the bear got the worst of it, although grizzly bears were not placed on the list of endangered species by the Department of Interior until 1975. Zenas Leonard, who trapped on the Laramie Plains, told of an incident there in which a grizzly suddenly rushed upon two trappers whose guns were leaning against a tree. Each grabbed his partner's gun, thinking it was his own. One gun had a single trigger, the other had two. In their confusion, instead of shooting the bear, the men ended up beating him over the head, with more damage to the guns than to the bear.

When he had recovered enough to travel, Jed Smith led his party through the Big Horns to the Wind River, where they wintered in the Dubois vicinity in a Crow village. A few of Major Henry's men from the Yellowstone joined them. Getting restless, Jed Smith and some of his men failed in an attempt to negotiate Union Pass in February 1824. Heeding Crow advice, they then slogged south 100 miles to South Pass where they took an intensive course in how to face wind-driven snow, known as ground blizzards in the West. This first party to go through South Pass westward (March 1824) included five men destined to rise to the first rank among mountain men—Jed Smith, Jim Bridger, Jim Clyman, Tom Fitzpatrick, and Bill Sublette. They and some less famous companions found good trapping on the Green and its tributaries. In June they met on the Sweetwater, where they made a bullboat out of buffalo hides stretched over a round willow framework, and loaded their catch. Fitzpatrick and two companions floated down the Sweetwater into the North Platte, only to capsize in the rapids of Fremont Canyon. Disgusted, they cached the pelts they could recover, then hurried on foot down the Platte to Fort Atkinson on the Missouri. After sending a report to Ashley in Saint Louis they obtained riding horses and pack mules at Fort Atkinson and returned to their cache to pick up the pelts.

Much encouraged by Fitzpatrick's report, Ashley decided to go to the Green himself. Piloted by Fitzpatrick, he left Fort Atkinson in early November with twenty-five men and a pack train of fifty horses, well loaded. Deep snow and intense cold delayed them. Many horses died. The Pawnee villages where Fitzpatrick had expected to procure food were deserted, making it necessary to eat horsemeat until hunters could find some game. At the forks of the Platte they finally found some Pawnees in winter quarters, with whom they traded for horses to replace the ones that had died. Following Pawnee advice, they went up the South Platte because it offered more wood for fuel and sweet cottonwood trees, the bark of which kept horses alive when grass could not be found. As usual on the High Plains in winter, travel conditions fluctuated between favorable and impossible. At times there could have been no progress had not buffalo opened trails along the river.

In Colorado they turned north to the Laramie Plains of Wyoming. Streams flowing out of the Medicine Bow Mountains, according to Ashley, were "richly stocked with beaver" that March of 1825, and the Laramie Plains were "endowed by innumerable herds of Buffaloe, Antelope and Mountain sheep." Such an endowment could not be counted on every March. While some men trapped, others tried in futility to open a trail through the deep snow of the Medicine Bow Mountains; they found it necessary to go north to Pass Creek before they could go west. Beyond Elk Mountain they turned northwest to the Great Divide Basin, where they elected to go west not far south of Stuart's track of 1812. Pools of water from melting snow made traveling through the arid basin much better than it would have been in summer.

Crow Indians stole seventeen horses. Some of the men chased them north to the Sweetwater before they gave up the pursuit. Without enough horses for the packs, some of the men had to carry packs through falling and blowing snow the next few days until, under clearing skies on April 19, they reached the Green some fifteen miles above the Big Sandy. Ashley noted in his diary the next day: "The men are and have been . . . the last two days without any Thing to eat & they are becoming quite uneasy under their privation." [6] Hunters relieved the tension by bringing in some meat the next day.

---

6. Dale L. Morgan, ed., *The West of William H. Ashley* (Denver: Fred A. Rosenstock, 1964), p. 106.

Ashley put his men to work trapping at once, for the whole purpose of making such a trip was to get pelts for money. He sent parties north, west, and southwest. He and the remaining six men made two bullboats, loaded them with trade goods and supplies, and floated down the Green. Before dispersing his trappers, Ashley had told them to meet him downstream on or before July 10 on the north side of a mountain range (Uinta) which could be seen on the southern horizon. When he reached the Uintas, Ashley cached his trade goods and surplus supplies at Henry's Fork of the Green and peeled a few trees to mark the place. Climbing back into the bullboats, Ashley and his six men explored perhaps 150 miles farther down the Green. Then, having had enough perilous river travel (Ashley could not swim), he bought horses from Ute Indians and circled west and north around the Uintas. He came within thirty miles of the great Salt Lake before turning southeast to the agreed-upon rendezvous area, where he found 120 men and a few women. Besides Ashley's own men, the gathering included twenty-nine deserters (some of them Iroquois Indians) from the Hudson's Bay Company and a few other non-Ashley, independent trappers. Ashley's caches yielded ample tobacco, coffee, sugar, powder, lead, knives, beads, combs, rings, and other trade goods, but no liquor. The only women present were Indian wives of the ex-Hudson's Bay Company trappers. With so few women and no booze there was less hilarity and more attention to business than at any subsequent rendezvous.

The rendezvous was Ashley's great innovation to the fur trade. The original system had depended on Indians to do the trapping, and white traders operated out of forts, or posts. But Ashley saw that American fur men could produce more pelts by themselves. Furthermore, the rendezvous avoided the cost associated with a trading post and the necessity of keeping a garrison. One of the side benefits proved to be the social and sensual enjoyments of the rendezvous. In a week or two, normally in June or July, employees and free trappers could turn in their pelts, get paid and resupplied, make new friends, enjoy the fellowship of old friends, and raise hell.

The mountain men reached the rendezvous after a year of solitary labor in the wilderness. They were starved for pleasure and behaved accordingly. The raw alcohol that was passed around served to release inhibitions even more. There were horse races and foot races, wrestling and fighting, gambling, duels, and grappling of squaws in lust and love. Often a trapper might gamble away his entire winter's work and then shrug it off. After several days the excesses would run their course, the self-indulgent spree would end, and the trappers would disperse to nurse their wounds and rest up for another winter.

Whether by intention or instinct, Ashley had hit upon a method that succeeded as long as the beaver pelts lasted in abundance. The rendezvous was held for sixteen years and only played out when the beavers had been hunted almost to extinction in the mountains.

If we ignore the number of men who lost their lives in his employ and overlook the absence of compensation for dependents, Ashley rates as one of the most successful fur traders in Wyoming history. His losses on the Missouri before he moved his operations to Wyoming would have driven many a man into some other occupation, but Ashley persevered. In Wyoming his luck changed, enabling him to pay his debts and make a small fortune. At Henry's Fork in 1825 he collected 9,700 pounds of beaver pelts worth $48,500 in Saint Louis.[7] Some of his men using pack animals transported the pelts through South Pass to the Big Horn River just below Wind River Canyon. Bullboats carried them from there to the mouth of the Yellowstone River where they were loaded on government boats for delivery in Saint Louis. Ashley knew in advance that an army expedition was scheduled to be at the mouth of the Yellowstone and would transport his cargo down the Missouri. Using water transport made it possible to keep his horses in the mountains where his employees needed them.

As soon as he had unloaded his cargo in Saint Louis in October 1825, Ashley organized another winter expedition to the Green. He sent Jed Smith and sixty men toward Wyoming with a well-stocked pack train. Smith encountered problems much

7. Morgan, pp. 136–137 and Notes.

like those that had confronted Ashley the year before. Without Ashley to drive them on, Smith and his men holed up for the winter at a Pawnee village on the Republican River in southeastern Nebraska. When Ashley learned that Smith's party was stalled on the Republican, he arranged to meet it at Grand Island on the Platte in April 1826 with additional men, pack horses, and supplies. The augmented caravan reached the rendezvous site at Cache Valley, Utah, twenty-five miles northeast of the Great Salt Lake, late in May. Since Ashley had not seen this site he must have selected and announced it the year before at Henry's Fork on the recommendation of trappers.

Even with fewer men in the spring hunt than planned, Ashley collected enough pelts at Cache Valley to gross $60,000 at Saint Louis.[8] A well-guarded pack train took the year's catch through South Pass and down the Platte. No one challenged its progress. Ashley's receipts in 1825 and 1826 not only covered his earlier losses, but also netted $50,000 or more of profit. Twice he had gone up the Missouri, and twice over the Continental Divide in Wyoming. Then he resolved to sell out and give up the strenuous travel. Three of his employees, Jedediah Smith, David E. Jackson and William L. Sublette, agreed to take over the merchandise left over after the rendezvous, pay $16,000 in beaver pelts at the next rendezvous, and order at least $7,000 worth of additional goods from Ashley. The latter agreed not to supply merchandise to anyone ''other than those who may be in his immediate service.'' [9]

Smith, Jackson, and Sublette were three remarkable men. Smith, who was now 27, and Jackson, about 40, had worked for Ashley since 1822; Sublette, who was 26, had joined Ashley in 1823. The young men, Smith and Sublette, had shared many experiences as they advanced rapidly to leadership roles. They fought together against the Arikaras in 1823, went west and wintered together on Wind River, went through South Pass together in 1824, and wintered together the following year at a Hudson's Bay post in western Montana. Jackson appeared in the limelight for the first time when he entered the partnership with

8. Morgan, pp. 149 and 152–153.
9. Morgan, pp. 149–151 and 158.

Smith and Sublette. He avoided publicity, rarely went back to Saint Louis, and concentrated on catching beaver. Jackson Hole, Jackson Lake, and the city of Jackson are all named for him; they lie at the center of the tristate area where he operated.

Sublette's brigade trapped north of Jackson Hole in 1826. One of his men, Daniel Potts, wrote a letter the following year in which he described hot springs, mud pots, and subterranean rumblings at the West Thumb of Yellowstone Lake. This letter established the fact that Sublette's trappers, including Jim Bridger, visited Yellowstone Park in 1826. Theirs is the first undisputed visit to that area, since some people doubt that John Colter got there in 1808.

Late in 1826, Jackson and Sublette must have met and decided what the partnership would need for the next summer's rendezvous, because Sublette and Moses "Black" Harris, followed by a pack dog, started out for Saint Louis on January 1 with an order for Ashley to fill. They went overland on foot, attaching snowshoes when necessary, and finding game so scarce that they had to eat the pack dog.

Jed Smith that winter trapped in California. With fifteen men he first explored the Southwest, crossed the Mojave Desert, and argued with Mexican officials in Southern California before going north to work the American and Stanislaus rivers. Then, leaving most of his men in California, he and two companions crossed the Sierra Nevadas and the deserts of Nevada and Utah. The Bear Lake rendezvous was already in session when they arrived. Smith's stories of hardship and peril no doubt surpassed anything that Jackson and Sublette could relate, and he was well on the way toward recognition as an explorer second only to Lewis and Clark.

The partnership prospered modestly, as did their supplier. Jackson and Sublette delivered 7,400 pounds of pelts to Ashley's agent at the Bear Lake rendezvous of 1827 and took delivery of merchandise valued at $22,447.14.[10] Smith's 1,500 pelts were still cached in California. By contract the partners had to pay their debt to Ashley in beaver pelts at $3 per pound. No ceiling, however, had been set for the prices Ashley could

10. Morgan, p. 173.

charge for trade goods, a partnership oversight; so Ashley profit was virtually assured while the partners and trappers got squeezed by rising prices.

Jed Smith continued his explorations, leaving the lucrative Rocky Mountain trapping to his associates. After the 1827 rendezvous, he returned to California, again by way of the Southwest. This time the Mojave Indians, who had seemed friendly the year before, killed ten of Smith's eighteen men in a surprise attack at the Colorado River crossing, and took the horses and provisions. Only exceptional courage, stamina, and luck prevented further loss of life. As in the previous year, Mexican officials in California suspected Smith's intentions and doubted his story that he came only to trap beaver, animals that meant little to them. The governor almost forced Smith to go to Mexico City to explain his business in California, but relented and allowed him to sell his beaver on the condition that he leave California. Smith then took ship to San Francisco, and moved slowly north from there, trapping as he went, and driving 300 horses and mules that he had bought at $10 each with the expectation of selling them for $40 or $50 in the Rocky Mountains.

Serious Indian trouble threatened repeatedly in northern California before exploding in July 1828 on the Umpqua River in southwestern Oregon. Kelawatsat Indians attacked Smith's camp while he was absent, killed fifteen of his men, and made off with horses, mules, and beaver pelts. In five years Smith had been involved in the three worst disasters of the western fur trade—at the Arikara villages, the Colorado crossing, and on the Umpqua. What a series of setbacks for the reckless, clean-living, Bible-toting Smith, whose base of operations was Wyoming, but who never learned that a bird in the hand is worth two in the bush. Rather than trap in Wyoming he searched all over the West for better beaver areas without finding them.

Hudson's Bay Company officials helped Smith recover some of his horses and pelts, and paid him to cover other losses, although no evidence linked the company with the attack on the Umpqua. After spending eight months as a guest of the Hudson's Bay Company, Smith and a companion left Fort Vancouver for Montana where David E. Jackson was reported to be.

They found him and accompanied him to the rendezvous at Pierre's Hole, where the three partners were reunited in August 1829.

Smith's two-year absence, 1827–1829, had caused him to miss the 1828 rendezvous at Bear River. Jackson and Sublette, however, had kept the enterprise afloat by gathering more than 7,000 beaver pelts, small lots of otter and muskrat pelts, and some castoreum. Sublette had delivered the year's catch by pack train to Saint Louis, grossing nearly $36,000.[11] There is no record of the number of pelts marketed in 1829 or of the amount received for their sale. Again, as in 1827 and 1828, only two of the three partners had been productive, Smith contributing very little, although his explorations won fame for him. Most of his activity must be written off as research and development—ill-starred efforts to find new trapping grounds.

Smith finally ceased to be a financial drag in the fourth and last year of the partnership. The three partners led more than a hundred men into eastern Idaho, south central Montana, and northern Wyoming. They fared well enough to warrant sending Sublette and Black Harris once again to Saint Louis in mid-winter with an order for goods and supplies. Sublette and eighty-one men on muleback escorted twelve wagonloads, drawn by mules, to the 1830 rendezvous at the confluence of the Popo Agie and Little Wind rivers.

Smith, Jackson, and Sublette now decided to follow Ashley's example, and go back to Missouri and seek safer investments. They sold out to five of their employees—Thomas Fitzpatrick, James Bridger, Milton Sublette (Bill's brother), Henry Fraeb and Jean Baptiste Gervais—who called their combination the Rocky Mountain Fur Company. Remarkably successful hunts (their best ever) in the fall of 1829 and the spring of 1830 had provided the ideal occasion for withdrawal. Prices of beaver were high, having almost doubled since 1822.[12] Sublette's train delivered 18,000 pounds of beaver pelts to Ashley in Saint

11. Morgan, p. 197.

12. James L. Clayton, "The Growth and Economic Significance of the American Fur Trade, 1790–1890," *Minnesota History* (Winter 1966): 214. Much of this increase must have come in 1825, since Ashley received about as much in this year as Smith, Jackson, and Sublette received in 1830.

Louis; Ashley marketed them for $84,500, taking a 2.5 percent commission.[13] Certainly the partners had left the Wyoming scene with a flourish. They netted enough to outfit themselves for a venture into the Santa Fe trade. Misfortune-prone Smith died at the hands of Comanches on the Cimarron in southwestern Kansas in 1831; Jackson tried the mule trade in the Southwest; only Sublette would return to Wyoming.

There was no guarantee of success for the Rocky Mountain Fur Company. Competition for the limited supply of beaver increased. Hudson's Bay Company brigades had worked the Snake River country hard and had pushed into the Green River Valley. In a report to the secretary of war, October 29, 1830, Smith, Jackson, and Sublette had warned that the Oregon Country, held jointly with the British, was nearly trapped out and would be completely exhausted were the British not stopped. The Blackfeet spread their depredations farther than ever. No longer content to stay in Montana, they were ranging all the way to southwestern Wyoming and Cache Valley, Utah. Smith, Jackson, and Sublette had lost eleven men to Indians, mostly Blackfeet, in addition to the twenty-five slain at the Colorado crossing and the Umpqua.

The American Fur Company, which hitherto had considered Wyoming beaver not worth the trouble, sent a brigade into the Green River Valley for the first time in 1830. Lucien Fontenelle and Andrew Drips, who led the brigade, had been in western Wyoming in 1827–1828, but had not been working for the American Fur Company at that time. Threatened on all sides, the Rocky Mountain Fur Company, as H. M. Chittenden put it, "carried on a wild and roving trade" during the next few years. It may be assumed, however, that they would have done less wild roving had they known where to find high-grade beaver country. The Rocky Mountain Fur Company may have had too many cooks. Unable to co-ordinate their activities, its owners marketed no pelts at all in 1831.

The Pierre's Hole rendezvous of 1832 was well attended by the Rocky Mountain Fur Company, the American Fur Com-

13. Morgan, *The West of William H. Ashley,* p. 200.

pany, several independents, and many Nez Percé and Flathead Indians. One witness estimated that there were five hundred whites and five hundred Indians. It was Lucien Fontenelle's turn to miss a rendezvous. To the satisfaction of the RMF Company, Fontenelle failed to arrive with the AF Company's supply caravan until the rendezvous was over.

The presence of friendly Indian tribes (Shoshoni, Nez Percé, and Flathead) west of the Continental Divide, had much to do with the success of the rendezvous system. Into this peaceful environment blundered a large village of Gros Ventre Blackfeet in 1832 as the Pierre's Hole rendezvous was breaking up. Battle lines were formed, with Bill Sublette directing the attack of the mountain men and their Nez Percé and Flathead allies. At least twenty-six Blackfeet, five mountain men, and seven Nez Percé and Flatheads died before the Blackfeet withdrew. It was the bloodiest confrontation in rendezvous country during the fur trade era.

Competition intensified between the Rocky Mountain and American Fur companies in the fall of 1832, the main battleground being in Idaho and Montana. Besides hounding the RMF Company men in order to share in the best trapping, AF Company leaders conspired to turn friendly Crows against the RMF Company and pirated some of its trappers. New companies, attracted by inflated success stories into a trade already overcrowded, received short shrift from the majors. Nathaniel Wyeth, a Boston ice merchant, and Capt. B.L.E. Bonneville, a French-born West Point graduate, organized companies and brought brigades into Wyoming in 1832. Both almost certainly would have been successful had they come five or ten years earlier. Both had marked ability and adequate financing. Both were thwarted at every turn, persevered, yet lost money.

After three years in the West, Captain Bonneville wrote his story but could not find a publisher; so he sold it for $1,000 to Washington Irving, who reworked and published it in 1837. The first edition title, *The Rocky Mountains,* was changed in later editions to *The Adventures of Captain Bonneville, U.S.A.* Since Bonneville's manuscript was not preserved, no one knows how much of it found its way into the book. Bonneville admired the

mountaineers and Irving wrote: "There is, perhaps, no class of
men on the face of the earth, says Captain Bonneville, who led
a life of more continued exertion, peril, and excitement, and
who are more enamored of their occupations, than the free trappers of the West." [14] Irving contrasted the mountaineers who
rode horses with trappers along the Missouri; the latter, he said,
"are less hardy, self-dependent, than the mountaineer." [15]
Likewise, said Irving, the mountaineers are "a totally different
class" from the trappers and traders who had worked on lakes
and rivers for the old North West Company.

The best-known rendezvous, thanks to Irving's description of
it, occurred on Horse Creek near the Green in July 1833. One
participant estimated that 250 whites and 250 Indians participated. Irving never attended a rendezvous, but he learned
enough about the one of 1833 from Bonneville to give a plausible description. He seems to have erred, however, when he
wrote that "each company found itself in possession of a rich
stock of peltries." [16] No one was making much money in
Wyoming in 1833 except Bill Sublette, a hard-driving entrepreneur, who had mastered all aspects of the fur trade. During his
partnership with Jed Smith and David Jackson he had worked as
a brigade leader and also had been the liaison with Saint Louis,
spending considerable time there. Although he himself set no
traps after 1830, he had continued to make money through interest, commissions, and profits on supplies.

By 1833 Sublette was beginning to share some of his profits
with Robert Campbell, who had first come to Wyoming for his
health in 1826. Campbell had worked for a few years as company clerk for Smith, Jackson, and Sublette before becoming
Sublette's partner in the early 1830s. Their activities extended
far beyond Wyoming. In Wyoming in 1834 they built Fort
Laramie at the junction of the Laramie and North Platte rivers.
In the same year they reached an agreement with the American
Fur Company—it would stay out of the central Rockies for a
year and Sublette and Campbell would withdraw from the upper

14. Washington Irving, *Adventures of Captain Bonneville* (New York: F. M. Lupton
Publishing Co., 1843), p. 23.

15. Washington Irving, *Bonneville,* pp. 22–23.

16. Washington Irving, *Bonneville,* p. 130.

Missouri. Also in 1834 at the rendezvous Sublette effected the dissolution of the debt-ridden Rocky Mountain Fur Company.

At the time it must have looked as if Sublette and Campbell, with their fort on the Laramie, and with the RMF and AF companies no longer represented at the rendezvous, would monopolize what remained of the Wyoming fur trade. Instead, Sublette and Campbell, like so many others, decided that Wyoming was not really their land of opportunity. They sold Fort Laramie to Fitzpatrick, Milton Sublette, and Bridger, who soon passed it on to the American Fur Company and began working for that company.[17]

Fewer people were showing up at the rendezvous with fewer pelts, and business lagged at Fort Laramie, too, until the buffalo robe trade developed in the 1840s. The diminishing supply of beaver pelts, because of overtrapping, coincided with lower prices because beaver hats were going out of style in Europe and being replaced by silk hats and coonskin caps.[18]

The last eight rendezvous were all in Wyoming. Gradually the fun and frolic faded. Robert Newell wrote of the final meeting in 1840: "times was certainly hard no beaver and everything dull." He must have been thinking of only the business aspect when he said that everything was dull because he added that Black Harris shot at him with murderous intent. Nor was it dull for the great Jesuit missionary, Father Pierre-Jean de Smet, making his first trip West, who spent a very busy four days talking to Flatheads and Shoshonis and giving "good, wholesome advice to the Canadian hunters, who seem to be in great need of it." [19]

17. For diverse interpretations of the complex maneuvers, see LeRoy R. Hafen, ed., *Mountain Men and the Fur Trade of the Far West*, 10 vols. (Glendale, Calif.: Arthur H. Clark Co., 1965–1972), 1:137–138, 145–147; and 7:95–96; Don Berry, *A Majority of Scoundrels* (New York: Harper and Brothers, 1961), pp. 351–354; and Dale L. Morgan and Eleanor Towle Harris, eds., *The Rocky Mountain Journals of William Marshall Anderson* (San Marino: Huntington Library, 1967), pp. 23–30.

18. Paul C. Phillips, *The Fur Trade*, 2 vols. (Norman: University of Oklahoma Press, 1961), 2:532. The panic of 1837 had little to do with the declining price of beaver pelts, which hit bottom in the 1840s.

19. Pierre-Jean de Smet, *Life, letters and travels of Father Pierre-Jean de Smet, S.J., 1801–1873*, ed. Hiram M. Chittenden and Alfred Talbot Richardson, 4 vols. (New York: F. P. Harper, 1905), 1:221.

In the sixteen years of the rendezvous no one attended more faithfully than Jim Bridger. He seems to have missed only the one of 1833. Bridger, who spent most of his life (1804–1881) in Wyoming, ranks as its number one mountain man. His exploits are legendary. His most significant achievements, some of which will be discussed in the next chapter, came after the fur trade era. Yet even in the fur trade he distinguished himself. He was a rawboned six-footer with the powerful neck of a professional wrestler, a fine sense of humor, and a profound knowledge of the region. His inability to read and write handicapped him less than it would have farther east.

Some of the more colorful events at the rendezvous had Bridger as a principal: Dr. Marcus Whitman removed a three-inch arrow point from his back in 1835 while many men watched in awe; William Drummond Stewart presented him with an English suit of armor in 1837; Bridger led a large company to the Popo Agie rendezvous in 1838, and some of his men serenaded four missionary wives. Bridger himself may not have participated in the serenade, although his name was the only one mentioned in connection with it. Mary Walker wrote: "Last night disturbed by drunkards. A large company arrived under command of Capt. Bridger. A no. of them came to salute us. One man carried the scalp of a Black-foot. The music consisted of tamborines accompanied by an inarticulate sound of the voice. They . . . fired and acted as strangely as they could." [20] Myra Eells was shocked even more: "Last night twelve white men came, dressed and painted in Indian style, and gave us a dance. No pen can describe the horrible scene they presented. Could not imagine that white men, brought up in a civilized land, can appear to so much imitate the Devil." [21]

Fewer than 120 white men attended the rendezvous of 1840. When the American Fur Company, sponsor of the gatherings since 1836, announced that there would be no more after 1840,

20. Mrs. Walker's diary is in the Elkanah Walker Collection, Henry E. Huntington Library, San Marino, California. Used with permission.

21. Clifford M. Drury, *First White Women over the Rockies,* 3 vols. (Glendale: Arthur H. Clark Co., 1963), 2:100.

most of the five hundred or so trappers and camp tenders who had been working in rendezvous territory in the early 1830s had already left the area, and others soon drifted away. Many went to California, New Mexico, or Oregon. A few went home to Canada, Missouri, Kentucky, or Virginia, where most of them had come from originally. They entered farming, ranching, business, mining and many other occupations.[22] A minority remained in Wyoming.

Prof. James L. Clayton has argued plausibly that the American fur trade was never very important economically and moreover was never primarily a far-western phenomenon.[23] With equal cogency Dale L. Morgan commented: "We have seen much loose writing about the 'incredible richness' of the Rocky Mountain beaver preserves at the time exploitation began. . . . Maybe the American West was rich only in poor man's terms." [24] Morgan described the Wyoming fur trade accurately—rich in poor man's terms. Semiarid Wyoming's beaver habitat was limited by the scarcity of water, aspen trees, willow trees, and brush.

In comparison with the national and international fur trade the amount of business conducted did not add very much to the gross national product, even though it was the major economic activity of the region. At its peak the fur trade's work force in Wyoming could not have exceeded five hundred men. H. M. Chittenden reported that the average annual value of the Saint Louis fur trade, 1807–1847, was only between $200,000 and $300,000, and the rendezvous was not the only contributor to that trade.[25] No more than 3,000 men were involved in all fur trade activities west of the Missouri, 1810–1845, and most of them earned barely a living wage. Camp tenders who made up one-third of a typical brigade received wages of $200 a year.

22. Hafen, *Mountain Men and the Fur Trade of the Far West,* 10:9–15.

23. Clayton, pp. 219–220.

24. Dale L. Morgan, "The Fur Trade and Its Historians," *Minnesota History* (Winter 1966): 154–155.

25. H. M. Chittenden, *The American Fur Trade of the Far West,* 3 vols. (New York: Barnes & Noble, 1935), 1:8.

Trappers on wages received $400 a year. Free trappers made more or less, depending on luck and enterprise.

Nevertheless, in poor man's terms, Wyoming got more than its share of recognition because most of the rendezvous were held on the Green River. More than any other state, Wyoming has been identified as rendezvous country and as the home of the mountain men. Books of fiction and public school textbooks have exaggerated the economic importance and the color and romance of the annual gatherings, 1825–1840. Overstated also has been the freedom, independence, and self-reliance of the trappers' life. Consequently many Wyomingites are still enamored of the mountain men. For some of their twentieth-century admirers the essence is simplicity, getting back to nature, getting away from the restrictions of urban life. For others it is the independence and self-reliance, the daring and courage, the don't-tread-on-me posture.

Outdoor leadership schools offer popular courses on how to survive in the wilderness using only what nature provides. Mountain man trails are being traced, marked, and mapped in many parts of the state. Mountain man museums at Pinedale in the Green River Valley and at Moose in Jackson Hole attract hundreds of thousands of visitors every year. The Green River rendezvous is re-enacted at Pinedale every July.

Several hundred professional guides and outfitters make a living by serving out-of-state sportsmen. They preserve traditions of the mountain men. Ned Frost, a veteran guide and outfitter, who is currently historian of the Wyoming Recreation Commission, proudly explains that he learned mountain man lore from his father, who learned from *his* father, who learned from Billy Whitworth in the Big Horn Basin in the 1880s, who learned from Jim Baker, who learned from Jim Bridger. Taxidermists, trappers, and big-game hunters complete the long list of Wyoming people who identify with the mountain men.

The beavers, meanwhile, have survived even better than the mountain men. Trappers cannot take them without special permits, and can get the permits only when the beavers flood roads, dam drainage culverts, or do other damage. When placed in acceptable locations the beaver dams and ponds regulate spring runoff. They conserve water, stabilize stream flow, reduce erosion, and provide excellent brook trout fishing. Thus fur trade and mountain man residuals were much in evidence in Wyoming in 1976 and, more than any other state, Wyoming is identified with the mountain men of the early nineteenth century.

Also, of some significance nationally was the fur trade's contribution as a safety valve, a temporary or permanent refuge for "enterprising young men" who had some reason for leaving home—bad luck in love, no job, boredom, craving for adventure, disgrace, the sheriff. Probably many men stayed in the fur trade only a year or two. The work was often laborious and otherwise disagreeable—lugging six or eight five-pound traps, wading in ice-cold water, setting traps at just the right place so the captured animal would drown before it could chew off its foot, skinning the victims in freezing temperature, or toting the heavy, wet animals back to camp. Tension must have been prevalent—fear of Indians, concern about the safety and welfare of the horses, worry about where to find another productive beaver pond. But, after a year or two, when the mountain man returned to the settlements, he had stories to tell and a certain swagger, status, and pride.

The fur trade has done more for Wyoming than for the nation. Virtually all of Wyoming's economic activity before 1840, except subsistence hunting, revolved around the trade. Much of what has been published about Wyoming in the past 140 years deals with it. And, as will be seen in the next chapter, a few mountain men were the exception in staying in Wyoming when most people passed it by.

2

The Trails Territory

Wyoming was a thoroughfare rather than a destination.
—*F. L. Paxson, 1924*

Wyoming has more historic, nationally important trails within her borders than any other state in America, and a greater portion of those trails are visible and unspoiled today than in any other comparable area in this country.

—*Neal Blair, 1976*

NEAR Guernsey, in eastern Wyoming, a person can stand waist deep in the cuts made by wagons going West more than a hundred years ago. The ruts made by the emigrant wagons rolling over the Platte River Road, or Oregon Trail, remain visible in many places. But their impact on Wyoming remains invisible. For very few of those thousands who passed through ever found any reason to stay.

Once South Pass has been discovered, it was inevitable that Americans would travel through Wyoming in great numbers. Why more of them did not stay was less inevitable, although there were reasons for their passing by. The first trickle of emigrants actually flowed along behind the waning band of trappers. Jason and Daniel Lee, in 1834, and Dr. Marcus Whitman and Samuel Parker in 1835, attached themselves to trappers'

40

supply caravans as they moved from Missouri on their way to the rendezvous. In succeeding years, a few others also went with the trappers.

The trickle began to grow both because of a push from the East and a pull from the West. The financial panic of 1837 left many in debt and with poor prospects of improving their financial situation. Furthermore, the travelers along the trail had heard many glowing, even far-fetched descriptions of life in California and Oregon. The settlers on the West Coast were aware that the country would really develop only with increased numbers of Americans to join them. They waged a campaign not only to attract more settlers, but to ensure that Oregon and California became states. So it was that midwesterners and easterners heard of a virtual Garden of Eden: a place where unbelievable yields of crops were grown, where the sunshine and balmy climate banished disease and ailments. Letters home were passed around from neighbor to neighbor, were read aloud at meetings, and were reprinted in papers.

Nor was the search for good farmland the only drive to go to the West Coast: the Indians were beginning to be converted. Or so it was, according to the report of the educated Wyandot, William Walker, who wrote a misleading account of the visit of four Indians to Saint Louis in 1831. They went East, Walker said, to ask the white man to convert them and show them the way to heaven. Methodists quickly organized to send missionaries to the Flatheads. Jason Lee went to Oregon, Marcus Whitman went to Washington, and these missionaries in turn bolstered the campaigns to bring Oregon and California into the Union.[1]

Conditioned by these images of paradise, few travelers were willing to entertain any thoughts about settling in a place like Wyoming. Who would live in the Great American Desert when a land of plenty shone in the distance? Who would join the mountain men in a life of Spartan hardship and dissolute pleasure when a great new society was being built beyond the

1. Ray Allen Billington, *The Far Western Frontier, 1830–1860* (New York: Harper and Row, 1956; Harper Torchbook), pp. 79–80.

mountains? With these impressions in their minds, it is no wonder the early emigrants saw Wyoming for what it lacked rather than what it had.

"This is a country that may captivate mad poets," wrote William H. Russell just east of South Pass in 1846, "but I swear I see nothing but big rocks . . . , high mountains and wild sage . . . . It is a miserable country . . . ." [2] One Chester Ingersoll commented in somewhat of a tautology on the other side of South Pass the next year: "This would be a delightful place if it were not so barren." [3] James F. Wilkins would not have made a good Wyomingite, since he called it "inhospitable, detestable country." Another plainspoken American looked at the landscape along the Sweetwater west of Devil's Gate and exploded, "Sand, sand, sand!" The migrant's-eye-view of Wyoming was summed up by A. M. Crane in 1852: "the whole region of the Platte is poor sandy soil and . . . worthless for agricultural purposes."

But the migrants were slightly prejudiced. Lt. Zebulon M. Pike and Maj. Stephen H. Long helped to tag the country as part of the "Great American Desert." Pike carried an easterner's bias against country that was not covered with trees; he regarded the soil as worthless because it did not support much foliage. After visiting the area of what is now Kansas, Colorado, and New Mexico in 1806, he reported that the country between the Missouri River and the Rocky Mountains was desert almost as far north as the Canadian border. He wrote that "These vast plains of the western hemisphere may become in time as celebrated as the sandy deserts of Africa." [4] The lieutenant may have been overimpressed with the aridity of the region because

2. Dale L. Morgan, ed., *Overland in 1846; Diaries and Letters of the California-Oregon Trail* (Georgetown, Calif.: Talisman Press, 1963), p. 609.

3. This comment is quoted from Ingersoll's Letter 5, published in the *Joliet Signal,* Sept. 14, 1847, and preserved in the Henry E. Huntington Library, San Marino, California. Much of the information presented in this chapter has been obtained from manuscripts in the Huntington Library; for instance, the quotations that follow in this paragraph, taken from Huntington diaries, which are used with permission.

4. Elliott Coues, ed., *The Expeditions of Z. M. Pike,* 3 vols. (New York: Francis P. Harper, 1895), 2:525.

he traveled through it in late summer when the High Plains streams run dry and the admittedly sparse ground cover loses its green color. Major Long underscored Pike's observations. He led a government expedition west through Nebraska and Colorado and back through Kansas and Oklahoma in 1820, saying the area was "almost wholly unfit for cultivation and of course uninhabitable by a people depending upon agriculture for their subsistence." [5]

It was actually Dr. Edwin James, the Long expedition's chronicler, who spawned the famous (or infamous) phrase "Great Desert." His account, published in 1823, included a map with the words "Great Desert" spread over the territory between the Platte and Arkansas rivers. James also gave his opinion that "the want of timber, of navigable streams, and of water for the necessities of life render it an unfit residence for any but a nomad population." [6] Later maps embellished the phrase. Thomas Farnham passed through Wyoming in 1839 and applied the term "Great American Desert" to the region between central Nebraska and the Rockies.

Wyoming bore the brunt of the overland migration, 1841–1868, because it was common knowledge that the route which followed the Platte River to west central Nebraska and thereafter its northern branch, was superior to the two best-known alternatives—the Missouri River for those going to the Northwest and the Santa Fe Trail for those headed for California. The Rocky Mountain barrier sags between the Wind River Mountains and the Sierra Madres in south central Wyoming and leaves an opening 100 miles wide in the form of the Great Divide Basin. South Pass is at the north side of that gap, separated from it only by the low Antelope Hills.

5. R. G. Thwaites, *Early Western Travels 1748–1846*, 32 vols. (Cleveland: Arthur H. Clark, 1905), 14:20.

6. Thwaites, *Early Western Travels*, 14:20. A general discussion of the Great American Desert idea may be found in Ralph C. Morris, "The Notion of a Great American Desert East of the Rockies," *Mississippi Valley Historical Review* 13 (September 1926): 190–200. Geographers' views of the subject are published in Brian W. Blouet and Merlin P. Lawson, eds., *Images of the Plains* (Lincoln: University of Nebraska Press, 1975).

The historian Merrill Mattes justifiably praises the advantages of "The Great Platte River Road." He regards the route from Fort Kearney in central Nebraska to Fort Laramie in eastern Wyoming as "the superhighway of westward expansion." The continuation of that road 300 miles beyond Fort Laramie is no less worthy of that designation. The Platte River Road was a highway, if not a superhighway, in the context of the nineteenth century when most U.S. roads had more hills, rocks, and mud, and required more preparation and maintenance. Emigrants who followed the Platte River and North Platte from the Missouri to central Wyoming enjoyed 600 miles of mostly smooth and mud-free road with access to water, grass, and fuel. The mud-free description is more appropriate for Wyoming than Nebraska because there was more sand and less rain in Wyoming. When the emigrants had to leave the North Platte in central Wyoming where it turned to the south, they found a convenient tributary, the Sweetwater, coming from exactly the right direction. It led them 150 miles west to South Pass, the least demanding of all Rocky Mountain passes, level and smooth, only 7,550 feet above sea level, sloping gently on both sides of the summit, and affording grass, fuel, and good water all the way to the summit.

The great thoroughfare through central Wyoming has been known by several names besides "Platte River Road" since the 1840s—Oregon Trail, California Trail, and the Mormon Trail, the last turning southwest toward the Great Salt Lake at the Parting of the Ways in western Wyoming, twenty miles west of South Pass summit.

Somewhere between 350,000 and 400,000 emigrants, most of them men, moved west between 1841 and 1868 along this thoroughfare which we shall call the Platte River Road. Beyond the Continental Divide, marked by South Pass, the emigrants fanned out along several trails according to their destinations. The traffic was greatest in 1850 and 1852, totaling 55,000 in 1850 and 50,000 in 1852.

Half of the emigrant traffic did not reach Wyoming at all in 1859 because it was diverted to Colorado as part of the Pike's Peak gold rush. Another bulge in Wyoming traffic to 25,000 or so in 1865 and again in 1866 resulted from gold discoveries in

Idaho and Montana and from flight from the Civil War and its aftermath.[7] Capt. Eugene F. Ware reported that the 1864 traffic, as he observed it in Nebraska, consisted mainly of draft evaders, deserters, "secesh," and people who wanted no part of the war on either side.

While westbound emigrants made up most of the traffic, many other people, traveling in both directions, mingled with them in the 1850s and 1860s—West Coast miners going to Colorado or back home, regular and volunteer army troops, stagecoach passengers, stationkeepers, mail contractors, Pony Express riders, freighters, livestock drovers, and telegraph company employees. The Pony Express riders, 15-year-old Buffalo Bill Cody among them, added special drama and color during the eighteen months, April 1860–October 1861. U.S. Sen. William M. Gwin of California and William H. Russell of the Russell, Majors and Waddell freighting firm promoted this fast mail service which took ten days from Saint Joseph, Missouri, to Sacramento, California. Russell hoped that favorable publicity would enable his company to obtain a large federal subsidy. Small men and boys, weighing no more than 120 pounds, served as riders. They changed horses at every station. In Wyoming alone there were forty Pony Express stations, 8–20 miles apart. Among the Wyoming stations were Fort Laramie, Horse Shoe, Bed Tick, Deer Creek, Red Butte, Sweetwater, Split Rock, Three Crossings, Pacific Springs, Big Sandy, and Fort Bridger. Each Wyoming rider rode about thirty-six miles (average) in one direction, passed his mail to another rider coming from the other direction, picked up mail from him, and rode back to the station where he had begun his day's ride.

Emigrants whose oxen lumbered along at two miles an hour envied the express riders who streaked past them at intervals. Favorable publicity notwithstanding, the government refused to provide the hoped-for subsidy, so the company lost money even

7. In this paragraph and the preceding one I have used data from Merrill Mattes, *The Great Platte River Road* (Lincoln: Nebraska State Historical Society, 1969), pp. 23–24. Mattes estimates travel during the years 1841–1866. Covered wagon travel continued on the Wyoming trails into the twentieth century.

at $5 per half-ounce letter, and the overland telegraph provided a much faster communication service in October 1861.

Without a few exciting diversions such as watching Pony Express riders flash by, the emigrants might have found Wyoming hopelessly dull. Most of them took between three weeks and five weeks to travel the 400-plus miles between Nebraska and Idaho or Utah and probably wished for a shortcut or no Wyoming at all. They grew weary of sagebrush and blowing sand.

Looking for farmland, the emigrants found none. Willing to stop for sudden gold or the promise of commerce at a navigable river, they found no such reasons for staying in Wyoming. The entire roadway through Wyoming took the emigrants past arid country: annual rainfall in the southeastern corner is fourteen to sixteen inches, and in the southwest gets down to eight inches (ten inches or less qualifies an area as desert). The earliest reports dwelled not only on the aridity, however, but the other dismal signs that travelers should keep a move on.

Travel along the Oregon Trail, at least in Wyoming, was not so much dangerous as it was monotonous. A typical day began at sunup, with a hot fire over gathered cow chips to cook breakfast. Then the caravan lined up, the scout or guide going on ahead to mark the trail and locate a stopping place for lunch. As the wagons got under way, the horses not being ridden trailed along behind, with the cattle and herdsmen smothered under a cloud of dust at the very rear. The oxen-pulled wagons moved slowly, and children could run alongside and make forays into the countryside. The wagons halted for a light lunch, and water for the stock, if it was available, then the journey got under way again during a sleepy and often weary afternoon. When the wagons at last reached the camping spot selected by the guide, the wagons turned into a circle and the cooking fire lasted into the evening as stories were told and plans were made for the future. And then the next day the same.

T. S. Kenderdine in 1858 found the forty-mile shortcut from the North Platte to the Sweetwater to be "a gloomy, God-forsaken country." [8] The scenery along the Sweetwater he de-

8. T. S. Kenderdine, *A California Tramp* (Newtown, Pa., 1888. Printed by Globe Printing House, Philadelphia), p. 78.

scribed as "a cheerless picture, made still more so by the numerous human graves." Ox carcasses and skeletons "strewed the margins of the road and made a vast charnel-house of the valley of the Sweetwater." Close to South Pass a windstorm blew sharp sand in his face, almost blinding him. Desert countries are notoriously cold at night; so it should surprise no one that Matthew Field on the Green River on August 16, 1843, wrote "Cold as January! ice at 6 and mosquitos at 8 a.m." [9]

The travelers on the Platte River Road missed seeing Wyoming's most spectacular scenery—for example, Jackson Hole, the Teton, Absaroka, Big Horn, and Medicine Bow mountains, Devils Tower, the Wind River Canyon, the falls and Grand Canyon of the Yellowstone River, and the geysers nearby. They glimpsed only a poor, south-end view of the Wind River Mountains. However, they found other, less spectacular natural features to write about in their diaries.

Laramie Peak (10,274 feet above sea level), though not to be compared to Gannett Peak (13,804) and the Grand Teton (13,766), impressed them because it was the first mountain they could see as they approached Wyoming from western Nebraska. Only twenty-five miles south of their road, Laramie Peak rose high above all other mountains in the Laramie Range, and was in view for more than 100 miles.

Farther along, almost all diarists mentioned Independence Rock, fifty-five miles west of present Casper, because so many travelers ahead of them had painted or carved their names on its gray granite sides that Jesuit missionary Pierre-Jean de Smet called it "the great register of the desert." Father de Smet added his own name in 1840. Thousands of others followed his example. Were it not for the names and for the rock's location adjacent to the road and 100 feet north of the Sweetwater River, the rounded rock's modest proportions would not have attracted much attention in the Rocky Mountains. It covers twenty-five acres and is 135 feet high at its highest point. Emigrants variously compared it to "a stern dome," a "bowl turned upside down," "a mammoth egg half buried," "a great turtle,"

9. Matthew C. Field, *Prairie and Mountain Sketches,* ed. Kate L. Gregg and John Francis McDermott (Norman: University of Oklahoma Press, 1957), p. 151.

"a huge, sleeping hippopotamus," and "a huge whale." The famous trapper-trader William Sublette celebrated the Fourth of July at Independence Rock in 1829, hence the name.

Five miles west of Independence Rock the emigrants passed a landmark which is inherently more interesting, Devil's Gate, a superposed canyon, where the Sweetwater River flows through a cut in a granite ridge 350 feet high. The canyon, which is 400 yards long, narrows to only 35 feet at its eastern end, just wide enough for the river to pass through. Sixty miles west of Devil's Gate many of the emigrants gathered around Ice Slough, which they had read about in their guidebooks. Each winter, water seeped under the sod in the slough and froze. Insulated by the sod, the ice survived until the last days of July. Many of the emigrants paused here to prepare cold drinks and ice cream.

Sixty miles farther and 1,100 feet higher, the travelers arrived at South Pass, the fifth of their most striking natural conversation pieces. Diarists expressed disappointment because the pass was so unspectacular, and satisfaction because negotiating it posed no problem. Father de Smet described the pass as "almost imperceptible," while the famous "pathfinder," John Charles Frémont, wrote that the ascent had been so gradual that he had to "watch very closely" to find the summit.

In between these diverting landmarks, trouble might overtake the emigrants at any moment. They had a favorite phrase which they used for especially painful experiences. They said they had seen the elephant. Perhaps the phrase originated in circus lore. When you had seen the elephant, you had seen the most a circus had to offer. Seeing the elephant on the trail meant that you had "had it." Some diarists said that they had seen the elephant's tail or his tracks, meaning that they had experienced a minor calamity.

Tribulations that, in combination if not singly, could bring out the elephant included wind, dust, blowing sand, cracked lips, mosquitoes, hail, cold, snow, no grass, bad water, no fuel, quarrels, fatigue, dead draft animals, broken-down wagons, illness, accidents, Indian attacks, and death. Many emigrants had trouble in crossing the North Platte and Green rivers. In June and July the runoff from the mountain snowpack made these two rivers too deep, swift, and cold for safe fording. Many emigrants who tried to ford or to cross on makeshift rafts found themselves embarked on the River Styx at midcurrent. During the peak travel years the drownings must have averaged one a day at each of the two major river crossings. Vincent Hoover recorded the difficulties he had in forcing his livestock to swim across the North Platte at present Casper in 1849: "We have done nothing but wade in the water, all day long. We have invented plans after plans, but to no purpose. We have stoned, hammered, and beat the oxen, but it was useless . . . ." [10] When Hoover finally succeeded on the fifth day, he conceded that his oxen had had nothing to eat for three days and were scarcely able to walk. Livestock waiting on the south side to cross had devoured all the grass for miles around. Small wonder that many oxen died along the forty-mile stretch of the shortcut between the North Platte and the Sweetwater. Vincent Hoover without a doubt saw the elephant.

Wyoming did have a resident population in those days, however. It was made up of mountain men and trappers left over from the early days, and Indians. Both groups were forgotten, but the Indians showed they could not be overlooked with impunity. The few mountain men that were left sometimes found work as guides for the emigrants, but the number was small—probably no more than 5 percent. The only emigrants on the Oregon Trail in 1841, seventy or eighty members of the Bidwell-Bartleson party, needed only one guide. In the three years from the last rendezvous in 1840, only three "retreaded" mountain men—Tom Fitzpatrick, Capt. John Gant, and Joseph R. Walker—did all the guiding required by the emigrants.

Some of the men found work as guides with Frémont's government expeditions in the 1840s. Kit Carson led Frémont in his first foray into Wyoming in 1842, was joined by Fitzpatrick in 1843, then worked with Walker when Frémont went to California in 1845. However, the mountain men gained some competition after a few thousand emigrants had traveled to the West Coast and became qualified as guides. Furthermore the reputa-

10. Diary, July 8, 1849, in Henry E. Huntington Library. Used with permission.

tion of many of the professional guides was not untarnished. Many seemed to have promised easy routes that the settlers in their wagons and with their families found difficult; and some were no doubt guilty of out-and-out deceit, taking travelers to the Wasatch Mountains and then pointing across the alkali wasteland of the Great Salt Desert and riding off to leave the wagoneers to their fate. On the other hand, many guides found their advice scorned and their work unappreciated. One guide was described as knowing "about as much of the plains as the plains know about him."

Qualified guides were unavailable for most of the parties setting out for California during the Gold Rush, 1849–1853. By that time, however, emigrants could consult recently published accounts of travel on the Platte River Road. With inexpensive guidebooks, a well-worn trail, lots of company on the road, and free advice at many places along the way, most of the emigrant parties thought professional guides were unnecessary.

The fact remains that most emigrants were just passing through—few were staying, few were tempted to stay, and the population of Wyoming remained very small during the whole period of migration. That Wyoming appeared to offer few rich agricultural areas only partly explained the phenomenon. And the attractiveness of the destination also fails to explain adequately why Wyoming remained largely vacant. After all, other areas that offered land for the taking were able to attract people. But perhaps in each case particular exceptions overcame the natural obstacles. In the case of Utah, religious commitment of an unusual community provided the staying power. In Arizona and Colorado there were gold and other minerals. In dry western Oregon and Washington, enough water for irrigation and a mild climate. Montana and Idaho offer the closest comparisons, although both had more gold and silver. There development was also slow, although Idaho received a boost from neighboring Mormons and then, too, it had the great Snake River. Montana, like Wyoming, remained remote and unpopulated for a long time—but then, Montana did not have the Platte River Road running through it.

The failure of towns and cities to develop along the Platte

River Road is more puzzling than the failure of settlers to take root in the countryside. Cities normally spring up on transportation routes, and that Wyoming had. But cities also require some kind of crossroads, typically, and Wyoming offered no north-south route, only an east-west one. Then, too, cities in the nineteenth century still had to be near sources of food. Given the primitive nature of transportation and the poor farmland of Wyoming and neighboring areas, the food was not available even if someone had wanted to build a city.

But few came to Wyoming with that sort of vision, anyway. The talent flowed elsewhere—into the steel industry, into railroad companies in the East, into commerce and industry and even into agriculture and into settlement of California and Oregon. What Wyoming had was a population that today we would call the "service industry," plus some small retailers. Many of the permanent residents of Wyoming served the emigrants in various capacities at trading posts—posts like Fort Laramie and nearby Fort Platte. The life of the trailside merchant, hectic and unpredictable, illustrates the tempo and quality of Wyoming in the 1840s and 1850s. In June 1849, for instance, overloaded emigrants flooded the Fort Laramie market with goods. They had taken along more than their tiring draft animals could pull. "Every description of property but teams was worthless," noted one diarist on June 14. Two days later another reported that "here we found plenty of provisions without money and without price . . . piles of bacon and hard bread thrown by the side of the road . . . about 50 wagons left here . . . trunks, clothes . . . boots . . . lead . . . spades, picks, guns and all other fixings for a California trip, in the greatest profusion." [11] On the same day Vincent Geiger found the American Fur Company's cupboard bare, which is understandable in view of the fact the U.S. Army was in the process of taking over the company's property.

Prices at the posts jumped up and down. On June 27, James F. Wilkins reported these Fort Laramie prices: flour, penny a

11. These two quotations are from the diaries of Joseph Warren Wood and Isaac Foster, respectively, in the Huntington Library. Used with permission.

pound; bacon, free; coffee, two cents a pound; sugar, ten cents
a pound. In 1850 Fort Laramie prices were back to normal—
flour and sugar, 50 cents a pound; whiskey, $8 per gallon.

Emigrants who liked a nip and could afford to buy it often
carried their own supply, making the saloon business uncertain.
The usual price for whiskey at trading posts was $8 per gallon,
$2.50 to $3 for a fifth, and 25 cents a drink, when it could be
bought for 50 cents a gallon or less in the Middle West. A trav-
eler in 1852 remarked on the presence of a peddler with boxes,
kegs, and a sign "Whiskey and Soda Water" at Independence
Rock. He was not doing much business. Stage stations, of
course, dispensed liquor. Teetotaler Horace Greeley in 1859 described their whiskey as "soapy, ropy, turbid . . . abominable
witch-broth." In 1860, Sir Richard Burton, traveling in a mail
wagon, carried his own whiskey keg, yet sampled the wares of
saloons along the trail. He had few good words for the booze he
bought in Wyoming, although it seems to have helped make the
food more tolerable. Mark Twain in 1860 called all of the thirty
or more meals served him in Nebraska and Wyoming "exe-
crable" except for one consisting of hot biscuits, antelope
steak, and coffee which he enjoyed at the Green River Crossing.

Small trading posts sprang up along the 150-mile stretch of
the North Platte between present Torrington and Casper. Each
had its small cluster of French Canadians or Frenchmen
engaged in hunting, trapping, trading, peddling, clerking, guiding, or gambling. Emigrants generally considered them to be
mountain men, although not all of them had fur trade backgrounds. At Deer Creek (present Glenrock), for instance, a
freighter in 1858 came upon "quite a considerable settlement of
French traders and Indians." He remarked, "These traders had
mostly a plurality of wives, which they purchased from their fathers with powder and whiskey, and which they put aside at
their pleasure as soon as old age has marred their beauty." [12]
Horace Greeley reported that the price paid for Indian girls in
1859 ranged from $40 to $80, about the price of a horse, he said
(although trailside traders wanted more than $80 for a good
horse).

12. T. S. Kenderdine, *A California Tramp*, pp. 76–77.

At Plante's Station on the Sweetwater in 1860, Richard Burton summed up his observations in regard to the many French Canadians he had seen up to that time:

> They are a queer lot these French Canadians who have 'located' themselves in the Far West. Travellers who hunted with them speak highly of them as a patient, submissive, and obedient race, inured to privations, and gifted with the reckless *abandon*, . . . enduring . . . merry . . . . I can only speak of him as I found him, a lazy dog, somewhat shy and proud, much addicted to loafing, and to keeping cabarets, because, as the old phrase is, the cabarets keep him—in idleness too . . . .[13]

One of the most colorful and energetic of the many traders was John Baptiste Richard (often written Reshaw) who had at least minimal credentials as a mountain man because he belonged to an old fur trade family in Saint Louis, and had come West in the late 1830s. Like many other entrepreneurs of the frontier, Richard was versatile. He worked for Sybille and Adams at Fort Platte, giving part of his time to fetching contraband alcohol from New Mexico, with which he stood ready to debauch any Indian who brought a buffalo robe. Sometimes he went north as a peddler. At times he concentrated on the emigrant trade at various posts such as Fort Bernard, Ash Point, Evansville, and Rock Creek as well in southern Wyoming. Parkman met Richard at Fort Platte in 1846, and described him as "a little, swarthy, black-eyed Frenchman . . . in the highest degree athletic and vigorous." He wore buckskin clothes decorated with porcupine quills and fringes. His long hair, parted in the middle, hung below his shoulders. His half-blood Sioux wife bore him six children, one of whom caused him much expense and grief.

Mrs. Margaret I. Carrington described the Fort Laramie store after she had shopped there in 1866:

> . . . the long counter of Messrs. Bullock and Ward was a scene of seeming confusion not surpassed in Omaha itself. Indians, dressed and half dressed and undressed . . . mingled with soldiers of the

---

13. Richard Burton, *The Look of the West, 1860* (Lincoln: University of Nebraska Press, n.d. Reprinted from original 1862 edition), pp. 187–188.

garrison, teamsters, emigrants, speculators, half-breeds, and interpreters. *Here,* cups of rice, sugar, coffee, or flour were being emptied into the looped-up skirts or blanket of a squaw; and *there,* some tall warrior was grimacing delightfully as he grasped and sucked his long sticks of peppermint candy. Bright shawls, red squaw cloth, brilliant calicoes, and flashing ribbons passed over the same counter with knives and tobacco, brass nails and glass beads . . . , and that endless catalogue of articles which belong to the legitimate border traffic. The room was redolent of cheese and herring . . . and smoke . . . while the debris of . . . crackers lying loose under foot furnished both nutriment and employment for little bits of Indians . . . . To all . . . Mr. Bullock . . . gave kind and patient attention, and his clerks seemed equally ready and capable, talking Sioux, Cheyenne or English, just as each case came to hand.[14]

J. S. Wilkinson found a quite different atmosphere at Guinard's store at the North Platte Crossing (Casper) in 1859. Guinard allowed only one Indian to enter his store at a time. A clerk would hold up a tin cup full of sugar, flour, or coffee and indicate with fingers on the other hand how many cups full he would give for the hide offered by the Indian. Apparently Guinard worried about security at his exposed location, something which seems not to have troubled Bullock at Fort Laramie.

The Indian wives of traders provided more than antelope steaks and sex for their husbands. These "marginal" women, as sociologists have called them, served as interpreters and peacemakers, kept their husbands informed of tribal affairs, and promoted trade. A wise trader selected a mate from a prominent, influential family, the daughter of a chief if possible. He did not entirely overlook personal characteristics. Trail diaries supply evidence for the belief that there were some real headturners among the Sioux maidens around Fort Laramie and among the Shoshoni farther West. Mini-Aku, whom Captain Ware praised in 1864, was one. She was the daughter of the great Brulé chief, Spotted Tail. Although she seems to have preferred army of-

14. Margaret I. Carrington, *AB-SA-RA-KA, land of Massacre* (Philadelphia: J. B. Lippincott, 1878), pp. 76–77.

ficers, she might have reigned in some trader's home had she
not died in her teens.

Unhappily, marriages of convenience, as some of them were,
too often did not endure. Many Indian women, after a few years
were thrust aside or decamped, and went back to their tribes. A
notable exception was "Madam Jack Robinson," who turned
up with her husband, one of Jim Bridger's trappers, at Sir William Drummond Stewart's 1843 re-enactment of the rendezvous. Matthew Field, the newspaper reporter who was one of
Stewart's guests, related that "Madam Jack," as he called her,
was a leader of Shoshoni fashions and displayed trappings on
her horse that must have cost Jack Robinson (Robertson)
$300—"the amount of beads and bells that hung about saddle,
bridle and crupper, was really dazzling to behold." [15] Jack
knew how to keep his wife happy, and she in turn adorned his
household. She was, said Field, the "greatest lady we saw in
the Indian country."

The most famous mountain man of them all, Jim Bridger,
was proprietor of a trading post in the southwest corner of
Wyoming. In a Wyoming public opinion poll in 1954 Bridger
was rated among the state's six outstanding deceased citizens,
and historians rate his fort second only to Fort Laramie in historical importance. Bridger found it possible to shrug off the
demise of the rendezvous. It would take more than a depressed
fur trade to dislodge him from the Green River Valley. He
maintained his accustomed place between white and red society,
keeping his lifestyle, and adapting to changing circumstances.
No polygamist, he married three Indian women in turn, a Flathead, Ute, and Shoshoni. When the rendezvous system ended,
he and his old Rocky Mountain Fur Company partner, Henry
Fraeb, decided to build a trading post on the Green a few miles
below the mouth of the Big Sandy. Construction was in progress in August 1841 when a Sioux-Cheyenne war party killed
Fraeb, who was with a hunting party on Battle Creek in the
Sierra Madres. Bridger, who had not gone with Fraeb on the
hunt, then took as his partner another old friend and veteran

---

15. Matthew C. Field, *Prairie and Mountain Sketches*, p. 142.

mountain man, Louis Vasquez, whose attributes complemented those of Bridger. Vasquez could read and write, came from an upper-class Saint Louis family, had a white wife whom he brought West, and had had experience as a trader on the South Platte.

Bridger and Vasquez soon abandoned the site on the Green and moved forty miles southwest to one of its tributaries, Black's Fork. They first built a post on the bluff in 1842, and then moved down to the river bottoms where in 1843 they erected what would become one of the most famous posts in the West. It seems likely that Bridger and Fraeb, and Vasquez as well, had been thinking mostly of trade with Indians and mountain men, because there had been very few emigrants up to that time. They must have thought of themselves as filling the void left by termination of the rendezvous. In 1843, however, when a thousand emigrants stopped at Fort Bridger, a new era dawned. A few weeks earlier, some men from the fort, on their way to Fort Laramie to pick up some goods for the Indian trade, had met the emigrants on the North Platte, and no doubt had told them what Fort Bridger had to offer.[16]

Bridger did not give up his fall and spring trapping, although fewer trappers joined him. The beaver and the store kept him busy so that he found little time for guiding. His fame as a guide came later (1849–1868) when he served remarkably well a variety of engineers, sportsmen, and army officers. After meager results trapping on the Milk River in Montana in the fall of 1843 Bridger wintered at Fort Union in northeastern Montana. While there he dictated a letter to Pierre Chouteau, Jr., (at the American Fur Company) in Saint Louis, who had been his employer in the late 1830s, asking him to supply Fort Bridger. Optimistically he assured Chouteau that emigrants would be "well supplied" with money and would be in great need of horses, blacksmith work, and provisions; and that the Indians would have "a good number of Beaver." Bridger and Vasquez thereafter occasionally picked up supplies at Fort Laramie, Chouteau's nearest outlet.

16. See *Annals of Wyoming* 35 (October 1963): 204.

The veteran mountain man James Clyman, who had left the mountains, returned on his way to Oregon and California, and visited Fort Bridger on August 31 and September 1, 1844. He judged the fort to be only "a temporary concern" for trade with the Shoshonis and Utes "which trade is not very valuable." [17] Nonetheless, Clyman's party exchanged all its wornout horses and mules and obtained leather clothing and moccasins. Clyman also described Fort Bridger as "the general rendezvous of all the rocky mountain hunters & trappers," who had been reduced, he reported, to less than thirty men. Clyman just missed seeing his old friend Bridger and his brigade because they had just left for California.

Joel Palmer came along on July 25, 1845, and wrote a more comprehensive description of Fort Bridger. He said it was a "shabby concern" which offered robes, dressed skins, buckskin clothing, and moccasins in trade for sugar, coffee, flour, powder, lead, knives, and other white-man products. Horses were available at $25 to $50 in trade. Cattle, sheep, and goats grazed in the meadows. The several branches of Black's Fork were full of trout. Cottonwood trees supplied abundant firewood and logs. Since both Clyman and Palmer arrived late in the summer, their failure to find the store well-stocked with provisions for the emigrants might be accounted for by high-volume trade earlier in the season.

Normally Bridger and Vasquez offered more Indian goods than white-man goods. Normally, also, Vasquez minded the store more faithfully than Bridger. The partners provided goods and services that were appreciated by quite a few whites and Indians. Yet they had a poor location for business in comparison with Fort Laramie because (1) most of the West Coast migration took the Sublette Road, bypassing Fort Bridger; (2) people going to or through Salt Lake City postponed purchases whenever possible; and (3) unlike merchants at Fort Laramie, they had little trade in buffalo robes and no trade with army troops.

The arrival of the Mormons in 1847 marked the beginning of the end for Bridger and Vasquez as traders on Black's Fork, al-

17. Diary, vol. 3, Huntington Library. Used with permission.

though several years elapsed before they had to terminate their activities. Bridger first met Brigham Young just west of South Pass, and in answer to a question told Young that Salt Lake valley was not good corn country. Bridger had grown up in Missouri and knew good corn country when he saw it. Had he known all the trouble the Mormons would give him, Bridger might have said much more to persuade them to go on to some point farther west. Soon after settling in Salt Lake valley, Young eyed the Bridger valley. It looked like an excellent site for a Mormon colony which could supply the needs of west-bound and eastbound Latter-day Saints traffic. Also, Young did not like Bridger's prestige among the Indians and some parts of his trade with them. Young had to bide his time, however, until after the creation of Utah Territory in 1850 and his appointment as governor and superintendent of Indian affairs. He took office on February 3, 1851. The territory, which was larger than the present state of Utah, extended east to the Continental Divide, and included Fort Bridger and several ferries which mountain men had installed at the Green River Crossing.

Young rejected friendly overtures from Bridger. He thought Bridger and his mountain men were turning the Indians against the Mormons. In turn, the mountain men refused to pay taxes levied on their ferries. Relations worsened in 1853 when Governor Young revoked the Indian trade license issued to Bridger and Vasquez by an Indian agent before the creation of Utah Territory. In August 1853 Young sent a 150-man posse with a warrant to arrest Bridger for allegedly supplying the Indians with arms and ammunition to be used against the Mormons. The posse could not find Bridger. After consuming some of his liquor, part of the posse attacked the mountain men at the ferries, killed two of them, and seized much of their property. Leaving Vasquez in possession of the fort, the posse returned to Salt Lake City in October 1853. Young later sent thirty-nine men to establish a colony at Fort Bridger. Confronted by a dozen belligerent mountain men, the Mormon colonists decided to settle instead twelve miles southwest, where they built Fort Supply and planted crops in 1854. Thus Vasquez, with timely

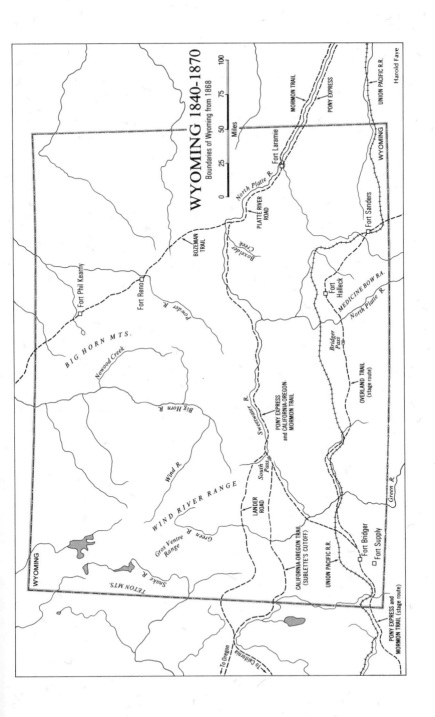

WYOMING 1840-1870

Boundaries of Wyoming from 1868

Miles

0 25 50 75 100

Harold Faye

MORMON TRAIL

PONY EXPRESS

UNION PACIFIC R.R.

WYOMING

Fort Laramie

North Platte R.

PLATTE RIVER ROAD

Boxelder Creek

BOZEMAN TRAIL

Fort Sanders

Fort Phil Kearny

Fort Reno

Powder R.

BIG HORN MTS.

Nowood Creek

Big Horn R.

Fort Halleck

MEDICINE BOW R.A.

North Platte R.

Bridger Pass

OVERLAND TRAIL (stage route)

Wind R.

WIND RIVER RANGE

Sweetwater R.

PONY EXPRESS and CALIFORNIA-OREGON-MORMON TRAIL

South Pass

LANDER ROAD

Gros Ventre Range

Green R.

Green R.

TETON MTS.

Snake R.

WYOMING

CALIFORNIA-OREGON TRAIL (SUBLETTE'S CUTOFF)

UNION PACIFIC R.R.

Fort Bridger

Fort Supply

To Oregon

To California

PONY EXPRESS and MORMON TRAIL (stage route)

support from the mountain men, held Fort Bridger, while Indian poachers and the short growing season drastically reduced the harvest at Fort Supply.

Meanwhile Bridger, after visiting Washington, D.C. in a vain effort to obtain relief, spent the winter of 1854–1855 at Fort Laramie, where the Irish sportsman Sir George Gore retained him as guide and raconteur for his luxuriously supplied hunting party. Bridger left Gore temporarily in June 1855 and returned to Bridger valley, where, after prolonged negotiations, he and Vasquez sold their fort to Lewis Robison, representing the LDS Church.

Another minor industry during the days at the Platte River Road was that of ferrying emigrants across Wyoming rivers, although the readiness of the poor and frugal emigrants to ford or make their own rafts, rather than pay high tolls, limited opportunities. A relatively small number of emigrants crossed the North Platte at Fort Laramie, and many of those who did were privileged to use a government ferry charging only $1 per wagon. The first commercial ferry at the so-called upper crossing of the Platte (at present Casper) was established in 1847 when Brigham Young assigned nine Mormons to provide service for members of their church. Thereafter the service was extended to gentiles.

In 1849, in a thirty-mile stretch of the North Platte, beginning four miles east of present Glenrock, there were several ferries, enough to drive the fare down to $2 per wagon. Each boat was made out of several logs, twelve or fifteen feet long, sharpened at both ends, dug out, and fastened together with poles and pins. At the peak of the gold rush in 1850 the fare rose to $5 per wagon. Silas Newcomb reported on June 14, 1850, that there were five ferries, each making a trip every ten minutes with an average load of one wagon and four horses. Operators would come from the states, install their equipment, stay long enough to make a few hundred dollars, and then hurry on, thinking that gold mining offered an easier way to get rich. Ferrymen could not survive year-round in Wyoming when their services were in demand only in June and July.

Two hundred miles west of the Platte the Green River had to

be crossed. Here, as at the Platte, several outfits along a thirty-mile stretch of river competed for business.

Some of Jim Bridger's friends who refused to pay taxes to Brigham Young appear as both villains and heroes in emigrant diaries. Dr. Edward A. Tompkins on the Fort Bridger route in 1850 reported "a miserable ferry . . . kept by vagabonds. . . ." On the other hand, an unnamed mountain man at the Green excited the admiration of W. S. McBride in 1850. He was a heavily muscled half-breed, more than six feet tall, "gifted with no ordinary degree of intelligence and energy." He defied bullies who tried to push ahead of others in line, and insisted that everyone cross according to priority of registration.

In the early 1850s the Mormons tried to monopolize ferriage on the Green through legislative action but encountered stubborn resistance. Sometime after the encounter at the ferries in which two mountain men were killed, Mormon ferrymen who turned up with charters from the Utah legislature were driven off by mountain men. The crusty mountaineers also sent packing a crew of Mormon bridgebuilders who arrived with orders from Brigham Young. The Mormons finally took control of the ferry business on the Green in 1855, about the same time they purchased Fort Bridger.

A few well-heeled residents built toll bridges in eastern Wyoming to compete with the ferries. Emigrants were willing to pay a bit more to cross on a bridge because it was safer, faster, and more convenient. John Richard, the trader already mentioned, and four partners built a bridge in 1851 over the Laramie River near Fort Laramie and another one over the North Platte near Deer Creek. High water washed out both bridges the following spring. Richard and one or more partners then erected a more substantial bridge at present Evansville (east Casper suburb) in 1852–1853. Richard soon bought out his partners and collected tens of thousands of dollars in tolls before Louis Guinard built a better bridge seven miles upstream (at present Fort Casper) in 1858–1859.

No bridge appeared on the Green until much later. When Frederick W. Lander, government roadbuilder, opened his new Lander Road north of the Sublette Road in 1858, he thought that a bridge was unnecessary, since the Green was smaller at his crossing. Later, when some of the emigrants had trouble fording, Lander recommended construction of a government bridge with a blockhouse for protection against ferrymen who might want to destroy the bridge, but nothing came of his proposal. Had the federal government, at the beginning of the gold rush, built bridges over the North Platte and the Green, free or with low tolls, no doubt the lives of many men and animals would have been saved, to say nothing of time and energy.

Among the emigrant needs that Wyoming's small resident population could supply, fresh draft animals and saddle horses were sometimes of great importance. According to Capt. Eugene F. Ware, who patrolled the Platte River Road in 1864 and wrote an excellent book about his experiences, western Nebraska ranchmen traded one road-ready ox for two footsore ones. In a short time the hoofs of the footsore oxen grew out and they were ready to be traded to other emigrants on the same one-for-two basis. While this no doubt happened, diaries kept by travelers on the Wyoming thoroughfare rarely mentioned one-for-two exchanges.

Considering the many dead oxen reported to be lying beside the trail there should have been great opportunity in the replacement business, but there was not. Apparently traders accumulated large herds, but could not turn them into cash. Most of the emigrants could not, or would not, pay the prices demanded. Some fitted their oxen with hide boots to protect their hoofs before they were too far gone. Many travelers had extra draft animals which they could substitute for worn-out ones, or they obtained replacements from other emigrants, or they got along with fewer draft animals by lightening their loads and shortening the wagon boxes. Sometimes they converted their wagons into carts, or abandoned their vehicles and turned to packhorses or mules.

Resident blacksmiths did pretty well. Many diarists complained about what they had to pay the smiths. One smith on the Sweetwater charged $6 for shoeing a horse and $12 for shoeing an ox in 1852, but the going rate was $1 per shoe, the emigrant furnishing the shoe. Diaries mention blacksmith shops at Fort

Laramie, the upper Platte crossing, Devil's Gate, South Pass, Fort Bridger, and Bear River. Jim Bridger had been a blacksmith's apprentice in his teens in Saint Louis, and had a shop at his fort, but seems to have spent little time at the forge. Some travelers mentioned that they were permitted to use his equipment.

There was money to be made by entrepreneurs who set up trading posts, ferries, bridges, blacksmith shops, and livestock exchanges along the Platte River Road, but not for more than a few hundred all told. Most of the entrepreneurs were almost as transient as their customers. Jim Bridger had been overoptimistic when he said in 1843 that the people on the trails "are generally well supplied with money." In fact, most of the emigrants were short of cash, and those who had money parted with it grudgingly.

A very large part of Wyoming's residents not only did not profit from the emigrants, but were directly harmed by them. The increase in traffic on the Platte River Road alarmed many Indians and worried thoughtful whites.[18] The pioneer settlers in eastern Nebraska and Kansas, hide hunters, and Platte River Road emigrants were depleting grass, timber, and worst of all, the Plains Indians' principal source of food, the buffalo. The nomads of the plains were being compressed into a smaller area. Their growing resentment threatened to explode unless something was done.

The westward migration of whites on the Platte River Road had begun in an atmosphere of apprehension. Jim Bridger, whose partner Fraeb had been killed by a Sioux-Cheyenne war party on Battle Creek in 1841, warned some of Frémont's men in 1842 of the likelihood of trouble, and Frémont's report in turn caused most of the emigrants to prepare for trouble that never came in the 1840s. The Indians were remarkably friendly in the 1840s and 1850s, considering the growing impact of white encroachment on their way of life.

At least 95 percent of the permanent and semipermanent residents of Wyoming during the great migration on the Platte River

18. From 4,000 in 1848, the number rose to 55,000 by 1850.

Road were Indians. Use of the adjectives "permanent" and "semipermanent" calls for an explanation. Semipermanent or transient seems appropriate for most of the Indians, since they spent much of their time outside of Wyoming. Just as the few hundred whites who catered to the needs of the transient emigrants varied from transient to semipermanent to permanent, so did the Indians. The number of Indians in Wyoming had doubled in the twenty years after 1834. The limiting factors that held down the number of white residents had also held down the Indian population. It will be recalled that the Wilson Price Hunt and Robert Stuart parties early in the nineteenth century encountered small parties of Crows, Shoshonis, and Arapahos. No doubt there were also some Cheyennes that they did not see. All four of these tribes were still in Wyoming when the emigrants came in the 1840s. And many Sioux, mainly Brulé and Oglala, entered from the Dakota area in the 1830s and 1840s. Fort Laramie traders invited the Brulés and Oglalas, who were located in the Black Hills, to move closer to the new fort. They came, and soon they outnumbered all other Indians in Wyoming. They probably would have come willy-nilly, since they were being pushed by other Indians. In the 1850s the immigrant Sioux drove the Crows, who had been in northern Wyoming for a century or more, into Montana. They also harassed and drove westward the Shoshonis who had been in Wyoming for two centuries or more. In their forays against the Crows and Shoshonis the Sioux often associated with the Arapahos and Cheyennes, who had been in eastern Wyoming for two centuries or more. In 1866 the Upper Platte Agency, Fort Laramie, reported that it had jurisdiction over 7,865 Brulé and Oglala Sioux, 1,800 Arapahos, and 720 Cheyennes. At that time there were 1,900 eastern Shoshoni in the Green River Valley, most of them belonging to Washakie's band. With respect to residency, the 1,900 eastern Shoshoni were definitely permanent. An equal number of the eastern Shoshoni were just west of Wyoming, and may be classed as transients as far as Wyoming is concerned, since they sometimes visited in Wyoming. Since the Brulé and Oglala Sioux divided their time between Wyoming, Nebraska, and Dakota, they may be regarded as semipermanent residents of

Wyoming. Likewise the Arapahos and Cheyennes were semi-permanent, since they spent a good part of their time in Colorado until they found life intolerable there in the 1860s and moved north. The transient classification is appropriate for the Blackfeet who had given the mountain men so much trouble in the 1820s and 1830s—they were domiciled in Montana and spent very little time in Wyoming. Transient is appropriate also for the Utes of Colorado and Utah, the Bannocks of Idaho, and the Crows of Montana, all of whom spent little time in Wyoming after midcentury.

Had the emigrants been asked at the jumping-off places along the Missouri River what they feared most about the trip in the years 1840–1868, most of them probably would have cited Indians. Most of them prepared for Indian attacks, which materialized for very few of them.

As for depredations along the Platte River Road, the Blackfeet and Crows were not involved, being far north of it. The eastern Shoshonis who occupied western Wyoming were generally friendly, accepting Chief Washakie's philosophy of co-existence. What trouble there was—and there wasn't much until the 1860s—involved the immigrant Sioux and their allies, the Arapahos and Cheyennes.

Two important federal government decisions resulted from the anticipation of an Indian uprising. First, in 1849 the U.S. Army bought and garrisoned Fort Laramie, as it had garrisoned Fort Kearney in Nebraska in 1848. The government had been considering placing troops on the Platte River Road for several years to protect the emigrants. Second, the U.S. Congress authorized a treaty council at Fort Laramie in 1851 to promote peace with the High Plains Indians. Tom Fitzpatrick, who had become the first High Plains Indian agent in 1847, and D.D. Mitchell, superintendent of Indian affairs in Saint Louis, had urged such a treaty council to head off trouble. Promising a general distribution of presents, Fitzpatrick and Mitchell invited all Indians of the northern High Plains to Fort Laramie for a discussion of grievances. Had they all come there might have been 50,000. Only 10,000 came, yet it was the largest assembly of High Plains Indians in history. They arrived at Fort Laramie in

September 1851. Finding insufficient forage for the horses, the council moved down the Platte thirty-six miles to the mouth of Horse Creek. The Indians, who were mainly Brulé and Oglala Sioux, Arapahos, and Cheyennes, accepted presents valued at $50,000 as compensation for past depletion of buffalo, grass, and timber. They agreed to accept $50,000 in goods annually for the next fifty years in return for permitting the establishment of roads and military and other posts. And they promised to keep the peace. To curb intertribal warfare, which had been more deadly in Wyoming than white-Indian conflict, the Indians were pressed to respect priority hunting areas—Shoshonis in western Wyoming, Crows in the north, Sioux in the northeast, and Arapahos and Cheyennes in the southeast. The Shoshonis were not considered High Plains Indians at the council but their enemies were urged to leave them alone.

Thereafter peace prevailed until 1854 when two officers at Fort Laramie mishandled a minor incident in which Sioux Indians had "barbecued" an emigrant's cow without compensation. Instead of paying the emigrant for his loss and withholding goods of equal value at the next distribution of annuities, an army detachment was sent to a Brulé Sioux village a few miles east of Fort Laramie to arrest a few Indians who were blamed for the barbecue. A battle known as the Grattan Massacre resulted when the Indians resisted arrest. This one-sided engagement, in which Lt. John L. Grattan, twenty-nine enlisted men, an interpreter, and one Indian, the Brulé Chief Brave Bear, were killed, caused the army to seek revenge in the Battle of Ash Hollow, Nebraska, the following year, in which eighty-six Brulés and four soldiers died. Although these bloody confrontations sent shock waves across the plains, travelers on the Wyoming thoroughfare were almost as safe in the later 1850s as they had been previously.

Making Fort Laramie a military post in 1849 meant the addition of many transient and semipermanent whites to the Wyoming population. In the years 1849–1868 the troops on duty in Wyoming, at Fort Laramie and elsewhere, fluctuated from 50 to 4,000 or more. Necessary support personnel—woodcutters, haying hands, laundresses, teamsters, scouts—added to the number of residents. Fort Bridger became a military post (1857–1882) when federal government difficulties with the Mormons prompted President James Buchanan to send troops to escort a gentile territorial governor to his post in Salt Lake City. Fort Halleck (1862–1866) and Fort Sanders (1866–1882) were built in southern Wyoming. Also, in the 1860s troops appeared at several points between Fort Laramie and South Pass to give additional protection to emigrants, stage stations, and telegraph stations.

In the early 1860s, hostilities on two fronts outside of Wyoming convinced the Sioux, Arapahos and Cheyennes that they must fight for their rights. In Minnesota the eastern Sioux killed 800 whites in an 1862 uprising and suffered equally bloody retribution. The western Sioux in Wyoming heard the bell tolling for them and launched attacks on whites wherever they were exposed. Meanwhile, Arapahos and Cheyennes in Colorado had been dislodged from ancestral lands and assigned to a small reservation which they refused to occupy. They joined the Sioux on the warpath, especially after the Chivington Massacre of 1864 in southeastern Colorado in which 150 Cheyennes and a few Arapahos were killed by Colorado volunteer troops.

Civil War priorities had left few regular troops in Wyoming. The Platte River Road had become so dangerous in 1862 that Ben Holladay moved his stagecoaches to an alternate route in southern Wyoming, the Cherokee Trail, so named because a party of Cherokees from Oklahoma had used it in 1849 on their way to California. This alternate route received a new name, the Overland Trail, from Holladay's Overland Stage Company. The Sioux, Arapahos, and Cheyennes thereafter harassed emigrants on the Platte River Road and the Overland Trail indiscriminately. They robbed and destroyed isolated stage and telegraph stations and pounced on small emigrant parties. Nonetheless, the westward migration continued, with small parties consolidating for better protection, and no one stopping in Wyoming longer than absolutely necessary.

Much inflammatory publicity, which was damaging to the Indian cause, followed a Sioux attack on a small wagon train at Boxelder Creek between present Douglas and Glenrock in 1864.

Three members of the party were killed, three seriously wounded, and two women, Mrs. Fannie Kelly and Mrs. Sarah L. Larimer, were carried off. Both of these women, after being ransomed, published books describing the attack and their captivity in terms which contributed further to white hatred of the Sioux.

Twenty-six army men, including Lt. Caspar Collins, were killed near Platte Bridge Station in the summer of 1865. Later that year, Gen. Patrick E. Connor, with 2,500 troops, made available by termination of the Civil War, tried to punish the hostile Indians reported to be concentrated in the Powder River country of northeastern Wyoming. Connor's army killed more than one hundred Indians, mainly Arapahos and Cheyennes, with a loss of twenty soldiers.

The government in 1866 built and garrisoned three small forts—Reno and Phil Kearny in northeastern Wyoming and C. F. Smith in Montana—in an attempt to protect travelers on the Bozeman Trail. This trail had been opened in 1863 to facilitate travel from the Great Platte Road in eastern Wyoming northwest along the east side of the Big Horn Mountains and then west to the Montana mines. But whites built the Bozeman Trail through what the Indians cherished as their last great hunting ground.

The Indians laid siege to all three forts before they had been completed and attacked all whites seen moving on the trail. Their most spectacular action occurred on December 21, 1866, when, led by the Oglala chiefs Red Cloud and Crazy Horse, they destroyed more soldiers in one hour than they had killed emigrants in the previous twenty-five years. They trapped and annihilated Capt. W. J. Fetterman and his entire detachment (seventy-nine officers and enlisted men and two civilian scouts), sent out from Fort Phil Kearny to repel an attack on a woodcutting detail. The dead represented about one-third of the fort's garrison.

Near midnight of the day of battle, Col. Henry B. Carrington, commanding officer at Fort Phil Kearny, sent two civilian volunteers, John "Portugee" Phillips and Daniel Dixon, on horseback to Fort Laramie with a request for reinforcements. En route Phillips sent a telegram from Horseshoe Station to Fort

Laramie, then, leaving Dixon at Horseshoe, he rode on, arriving at Fort Laramie late Christmas night, four days and 235 miles out of Fort Phil Kearny. Phillips earned his $300 pay, for no other ride in Wyoming history compares with his through dangerous Indian country in December 1866.

Reinforcements reached Fort Phil Kearny in January 1867, but all efforts failed to keep the Bozeman Trail open. In the Wagon Box Fight, August 2, 1867, five miles northwest of the fort, Maj. J. N. Powell with thirty-two men drove off a much larger Sioux force. Powell lost three men and killed an estimated sixty of the enemy.

But why were Indians and whites killing each other over land that neither wanted to live in? The area where the battles took place did not contain agricultural land that might support large populations. The Wagon Box Fight and the wipeout of Fetterman and his men took place near Sheridan—hardly a metropolis by any standard. Standing at the top of the ravine where Fetterman and his men fell on a cold December day in 1866, one can today look out over distant vistas of rolling hills. The only sign of the contemporary world is an interstate highway running a few miles away, or an occasional jetstream overhead. Here Crazy Horse mercilessly slaughtered his enemy, here the young men in blue died and were mutilated far from home. For what? It is not at all clear. Neither whites nor Indians could make much of the land, and it remains much as it was then.

The two societies were fighting in Wyoming despite the fact that the sources of conflict lay far away. Whites coveted the fertile farmland in Minnesota and the gold and silver in Colorado. Indians were standing in the way, and they were shunted into Wyoming, into a corner. It was a corner they could live with, at least until it became clear the buffalo were being killed out, and until whites continued to press for transportation routes across the corner itself.

The Indian-white fights were not over control of territory— Wyoming just happened to be the place where the disputes between the two societies were settled. And the battles themselves symbolize the many differences between the two societies. They were a small portent of wars to come, when mobility would become more important than size of force, and success would depend on the ability to live off the surrounding landscape. The battles typically ended in a showdown, but they were running fights, cavalry battles where the feint and the decoy were used to great advantage, and instinct and native intelligence played a more significant role than rationality and formal education. Fighting Indians was frustrating for the U.S. Army because redmen typically sacrificed their men very sparingly. There would be no massive rush where firepower could be concentrated—unless it was at the end, when it would be too late for the whites. But Indians also failed to exploit the weakness of their enemy—the long baggage train in the rear, vulnerable to attack, the inability to forage off the countryside. War became an extension of the different ways the societies had in thinking, in organizing themselves, in valuing life and property.

Only Indians and mountain men had been interested in making their homes in Wyoming in the 1840s. Twenty years later, after 350,000 people had inspected a strip extending from border to border the white residents included only a few hundred traders and their employees, support personnel for transient army troops, and a few Mormon colonists. The traders and support staff included some of the old mountain men. Wyoming's desert reputation persisted, though Horace Greeley modified it slightly in 1859. After crossing Wyoming from east to west he wrote in his *New York Tribune* that the Great American Desert terminated near the Utah line at Fort Bridger. The country between Fort Bridger and Salt Lake City, he reported, was neither fertile nor productive but had too much grass for classification as desert.

Committed though the emigrants were to locating elsewhere, they nonetheless contributed more to bringing about the creation of Wyoming Territory than did the odd assortment of settlers strung out along the Platte River Road. The emigrants were joined on the West Coast by a comparable number who had gone there by sea. Together they and their children wanted a transcontinental railroad. With the aid of powerful interests in the East they obtained passage of the Pacific Railway Acts of

1862 and 1864. The railroad builders a few years later brought enough settlers to warrant the creation of Wyoming Territory.

Once again Wyoming proved more attractive as a thorough-fare than a destination. No one wanted to live in Wyoming—they just wanted to pass over the ground because it led some-where else. Settlers looked at bare Nebraska and saw future cornfields and feedlots. They looked at a Texas terrain of flat, bare plains and envisioned enormous herds of cattle. They even saw promise in the sterile slopes of the Rocky Mountains of Colorado. But Wyoming—why, a fine place for a road to Oregon. A fine level route for a railroad. But not a place for sinking roots, for building homes and schools and churches, for making a community or building a new society.

The railroad focused national attention on Wyoming as never before and rarely since. In November 1867 the first Union Pacific train reached Cheyenne, where it was greeted by a great throng of bearded, longhaired men and a few women and children. Cheyenne had grown from nothing in July 1867 to 4,000 people while it waited for the first train, and 2,000 more people were added within the next two or three weeks. The city consisted of a cluster of tents, shacks, and a few rows of false-front commercial buildings set on a treeless, windswept prairie.

During 1868 track was laid all the way across southern Wyoming to the Utah line, more than 400 miles from Cheyenne. On May 10, 1869, the first transcontinental railway was completed with the joining of the Union Pacific and Central Pacific tracks at Promontory Summit, Utah.

Six thousand men—surveyors, graders, bridgebuilders, track layers, train crews, tie-hacks, and stone quarrymen—participated in the Union Pacific construction work in Wyoming. Ten thousand other people came to found a series of communities along the railroad—the larger ones being Cheyenne, Laramie, Benton, Green River, Bryan, Bear River City, and Evanston. Cheyenne, Laramie, and Benton had military garrisons in the suburbs. Each city inflated and deflated as the construction crews passed by. Each resembled bedlam at the peak of its population curve. When the flock of transients, the "Hell on

Wheels'' crowd, had followed the construction workers to the next end-of-track town, those who stayed behind worried about the future of their shrinking community. Benton and Bear River City survived only a few months, Bryan not much longer. Coal mining began in a small way at Carbon, Rock Springs, and Almy (near Evanston). The only settlements off the railroad were small ones at a few military posts and a larger one of perhaps 1,500 people in South Pass where traces of gold had been reported from time to time and a rush had come in 1867. Scattered individuals along the Great Platte Road rounded out the white population.

For the first time in American history the construction of a railroad preceded rather than followed the creation of a new territory. Most of the Wyoming country had been the western part of a large Dakota Territory, 1864–1868. Suddenly the western part of Dakota had many more people than the eastern part. In the middle of the territory, and separating the two parts which were occupied by whites, were close to 15,000 Sioux. Confronted by the dismal prospect that the unruly westerners would soon dominate the territory, the legislature in Yankton, more than 500 miles from Cheyenne, petitioned the U.S. Congress to divide Dakota and create a new territory, which it did with little opposition, July 25, 1868. Cheyenne people and Union Pacific lobbyists had also been urging such action, one of the lobbyists promising that Wyoming would have 60,000 people within one year. To make the new territory rectangular, eastern parts of Utah and Idaho were transferred to Wyoming.

Congressman James M. Ashley of Ohio had introduced a bill to create Wyoming Territory in January 1865. That bill died in committee. The name, however, survived and was sometimes applied to the area thereafter. In other bills, which were introduced in 1866, 1867, and 1868, the name ''Lincoln'' appeared in place of Wyoming. Sen. Richard Yates of Illinois introduced the successful bill in March 1868. However, the name ''Lincoln'' in the Yates bill was dropped after it had been pointed out that up to that time no state had been named for a president of the United States, and a territory should have a name that would be carried over into statehood. Before the

senators agreed on the name Wyoming, some of them who
preferred local names mentioned Platte, Big Horn, Yellowstone,
Sweetwater, Arapaho, Cheyenne, Pawnee, Sioux, and Shoshoni.

It is not known why Ashley, who first proposed the name
Wyoming, had selected it. Presumably he borrowed it from the
Wyoming Valley in the northeastern corner of his native state,
Pennsylvania. The pioneers there had obtained the name from
the language of the Delaware Indians, original occupants of the
Wyoming Valley. In the U.S. Senate debate in 1868 it was
explained that Wyoming meant ''at the big plains'' or ''on the
great plain.'' It was argued also that the name was euphonious,
beautiful, and easy to spell. The senators apparently made their
choice without consulting the residents of the territory, except
for a few lobbyists.

The organization of Wyoming Territory had to be postponed
until May 1869, ten months after its creation, because President
Andrew Johnson's appointees—governor, secretary, judges, and
others—were not confirmed by the U.S. Senate. Not until after
his successor, President U. S. Grant, had assumed office on
March 4, 1869, and his appointees had been confirmed, could
the wheels of government in the new territory turn properly, although Dakota had provided a few essential services in the in-
terim.

Meanwhile much had happened on the Indian front since the
Wagon Box Fight of August 1867. One of the most famous of
all Indian treaties was signed at Fort Laramie in April 1868, the
''Treaty with the Sioux—Brulé, Oglala, Miniconjou, Yank-
tonai, Hunkpapa, Blackfeet, Cuthead, Two Kettle, Sans Arc,
and Santee—and Arapaho, 1868.'' The federal government
wanted to move the Indians north, away from the railroad. So
the Sioux and Arapahos were assigned reservations in the western half of what is now South Dakota. Also the area north of the
North Platte River and east of the Big Horn Mountains—about
one-fourth of Wyoming—was set aside as ''unceded Indian territory,'' in which the natives might hunt freely as long as
enough buffalo remained ''to justify the chase.'' It was agreed
further that the Bozeman Trail and the three forts along it would

be abandoned. The Bozeman Trail was expendable since the Union Pacific would soon be able to carry people and freight to Utah, from where they could be transported straight north to the Montana mines. Some of the more suspicious Sioux, Red Cloud in particular, did not sign the treaty until November 1868, after all troops had been withdrawn from the unceded Indian country, and the Indians had burned the hated forts.

Another treaty was signed at Fort Bridger, July 3, 1868. Washakie's band of eastern Shoshoni, now reduced to about a thousand, agreed to move from the path of the railroad to the Wind River Reservation east of South Pass, 100 miles north of the railroad. A few hundred Bannocks also agreed to go to the Wind River Reservation, but elected later to settle on an Idaho reservation instead.

Thus Wyoming, if the 1868 treaties were enforced, would have no Indian wards except the eastern Shoshoni who obeyed Washakie, as soon as the buffalo were gone from the Powder River country. Whites along the Union Pacific applauded the assignment of Sioux and Arapahos to a reservation outside Wyoming, but they objected vehemently to having the Powder River country designated as unceded Indian country. They suspected that many of the Indians would spend much of their time in Wyoming, and could not be confined to its northeastern quarter. They were right. The Arapahos, for instance, fought Shoshonis and a U.S. cavalry company under Capt. A. E. Bates on the headwaters of Nowood Creek in the Big Horn Basin on July 4, 1874.

Eventually, however, in 1877 all Indians except Washakie's Shoshonis were driven out of Wyoming. An exception was made early in 1878 when 938 Northern Arapaho, unhappy among the Sioux at Pine Ridge in Dakota, were permitted to join their recent enemies, the Shoshonis, on the Wind River Reservation. Washakie protested, but not vigorously enough to halt the transaction. That ended the major uncertainties with respect to the location of Indians in Wyoming.

The Union Pacific was a key factor in the crucial changes of the 1860s. It brought close to 16,000 people to the Great American Desert, which settlers previously had shunned except for use as a corridor. It hastened the creation of Wyoming Territory. It expedited the removal of most of the Indians to Dakota reservations. Rarely has a railroad effected such revolutionary changes in any part of the United States in such a short time.

The desert notion survived. Indicative of its vitality was Congressman Ashley's 1868 statement in opposition to the act creating Wyoming Territory. Ashley had favored territorial organization until he had crossed the land to be included. His first-hand observation persuaded him that "not one acre in a thousand can be irrigated" and that without irrigation the area could not support the population necessary for a viable territory. The Union Pacific offered eastern people a chance to see the country for themselves but apparently that opportunity alone would not dispel the desert notion. The emigrants on the Platte River Road had not been impressed enough to stop. Would the same be true of train passengers? Would the Union Pacific be a bridge carrying people over Wyoming without leaving any of them?

At twenty miles an hour train passengers by the thousands rolled through country more barren than the covered wagon emigrants had seen along the Platte River Road. The *New York Times* in 1869 published one correspondent's account of what he had seen west of the Laramie Plains:

> what a scene of desolation met our view and surrounded us, that whole day's journey. . . . Here is indeed the Great American Desert—a vast barren basin, utterly destitute of life, devoid of living streams, a Sahara without a single relieving oasis, truly, the Valley of the Shadow of Death! I had been anxious to see sage brush, of which I had read so much; here it was in hideous profusion, a sort of devil's herbage whereof no living creature may eat. I had also wanted to visit the Alkali Plains—and here *they* were, stretching out in their white barrenness, altogether unlovely to the human vision! [19]

Amid such discouraging publicity the boomers in the railroad towns desperately sought to attract industry and people. In their extremity some of their leaders approved a scheme which gave Wyoming the unique distinction of being the Equality State.

19. *New York Times,* June 28, 1869, p. 2, col. 2.

3

The Equality State

*For fifty years Wyoming served as the leaven which
lightened the prejudices of the entire world.*

—*Carrie Chapman Catt, 1923*

EVER since the 1840s many women and a few men had
been working for woman suffrage in eastern states. They paid
little attention to the West, and were much surprised when
Wyoming Territory granted women the right to vote and hold
office in December 1869. The territory's very first legislature,
without much debate and with very little official record of what
was said, passed the revolutionary measure.

A few women of property had voted in New Jersey during the
years 1776–1807, and women in a few other places had voted in
municipal and school elections, but no government in the world
had given women full rights to vote and hold office before
Wyoming did so in 1869.

The famous "Act to Grant to the Women of Wyoming the
Right of Suffrage, and to Hold Office" is brief and relatively
free from ambiguity:

Be it enacted by the Council and House of Representatives of the
Territory of Wyoming:
Sec. 1. That every woman of the age of twenty-one years residing
in this territory, may at every election to be holden under the

laws thereof, cast her vote. And her rights to the elective franchise and to hold office shall be the same under the election laws of the territory, as those of electors.

Sec. 2. This act shall take effect and be in force from and after its passage.[1]

The legislature that passed the suffrage bill was in itself rather remarkable. It was small, having only nine members in the council (upper house) and twelve in the house of representatives.[2] Every member of the legislature was a Democrat. Only one member, S. M. Curran of Carbon County, speaker of the house, had served before in a legislature. Every member lived in a town or city, for very few people except Indians lived in the rural areas. The 1870 census would list only 165 persons employed in agriculture.

William H. Bright, a 45-year-old saloonkeeper from South Pass City, introduced the bill. He had never gone to school and said he did not remember where he had learned to read and write. A native of Virginia, he had served with the rank of major in the Quartermaster Corps in Washington, D.C., during the Civil War. In 1867 he and his wife, twenty years his junior, moved to Salt Lake City, where he worked as a U.S. postal inspector. He left that position and joined a small gold rush to South Pass in 1868, where, judging from the 1870 county tax roll entries, he did not do very well financially. His saloon, cabin, and personal property were valued at only $658.

"Colonel" Bright, as he was known, later said that he introduced the suffrage bill because he thought that women like his wife and mother had as much right to suffrage as the black men who had recently received the franchise. At another time he said: "I have never thought much about it, nor have I been converted by a woman's lecture or newspaper, for I never heard a woman speak from the rostrum and never read *The Revolu-*

1. General Laws, Memorials and Resolutions of the Territory of Wyoming, passed at the First Session of the Legislative Assembly, convened at Cheyenne, October 12, 1869, and adjourned sine die, December 11, 1869 (Cheyenne, 1870), 371.

2. A thirteenth member who had been elected to the lower house never appeared to take his seat.

tion. I knew that it was a new issue, and a live one, and with a strong feeling that it was just, I determined to use all influence in my power to have the bill passed." [3]

Although considerations of justice probably influenced some of the legislators, the majority approved the bill mainly because of its presumed public relations value. They thought that it would advertise the territory and attract population. They were distressed by the drop in population that had followed completion of the transcontinental railroad (May 10, 1869) from an estimated 16,000 in the summer of 1868 to 8,014 in June 1869, when a special census was taken. There is no reason to think that there was any significant increase between June 1869, when the special census was taken for legislative apportionment purposes, and December, when women suffrage was adopted.

In the fall of 1869 it became apparent that it would take more than a railroad to make a successful territory in the Great American Desert. The railroad began to look more and more like the Platte River Road of the previous generation, in that it gave tens of thousands of people an opportunity to see a strip of semiarid country but did not bring many settlers to the territory. So the Union Pacific became a bridge, as far as Wyoming was concerned, and a grave disappointment to the growth-seeking residents.

Many residents, including Gov. John A. Campbell, assumed that Wyoming must have great reserves of natural resources, which would require only people and capital for their discovery and development. Arguing that immigration was of the greatest importance, the governor in his opening address to the legislature urged the creation of an immigration commission with authority to collect and disseminate statistics about the resources of the territory. Rather than appropriate money for an immigration bureau, the legislators accepted the argument that adoption of woman suffrage would serve the same purpose at no expense.

The notion that woman suffrage would attract people did not originate in Wyoming; it had already been discussed in the U.S. Congress. George W. Julian, a suffragist and member of the

3. *Revolution* 5 (January 13, 1870): 21.

House from Indiana, had introduced a bill in 1868 to give women the franchise in all of the territories. In a committee hearing on the bill in January 1869 a witness lamented the excess of females in the East and their scarcity in the West. The opportunity to vote in the West, he suggested, would correct the imbalance. Although Julian's bill failed to pass, metropolitan newspapers gave space to the novel argument which had been used to support it.

The suffragist Edward M. Lee, secretary of Wyoming Territory, recognized the argument's possibilities, carried it to Wyoming, and capitalized on it. Lee was a 32-year-old bachelor who had served as a Union officer in the Civil War, and then had practiced law in Connecticut until appointed secretary of Wyoming Territory by President U.S. Grant. As a member of the Connecticut legislature in 1867, Lee had introduced a woman suffrage amendment. Although his bid had failed in Connecticut, his reform zeal did not abate. He knew that it was much easier to win suffrage in a territory than in a state. In a state the constitution had to be amended, which normally required approval by a two-thirds majority of both houses of the legislature and also approval by a majority of all the voters in a popular election. In a territory, on the other hand, the deed could be accomplished by a simple majority vote of the legislature and the approval of the governor, without a vote of the people.

Lee was Wyoming's most conspicuous suffragist as long as he remained in the territory, which was less than two years. Suffragists, male and female, were rare. Wyoming women in 1869 did not speak in public, had no suffrage organization, and limited their expressions of suffrage sentiment to private conversation. Lee presented his prosuffrage views in editorials in the newspaper which he and his brother-in-law published in Cheyenne. When a prominent eastern lecturer, Anna Dickinson, spoke on the subject in Cheyenne in September 1869, just a few weeks before the legislature met, it was Lee who introduced her.

Neither Lee nor Bright needed the attract-population argument to convince themselves of the wisdom of adopting woman suffrage, but did need it to persuade some of the legislators who paid little attention to justice arguments. Without the public relations angle, Wyoming's first legislature almost certainly would not have approved the suffrage bill.

Bright announced his intention to introduce a woman suffrage bill on the 27th day of the 50-day legislative session and introduced it on the 42nd day. It was his only bill. As president of the nine-man council he preferred to work with bills presented by the other members. Lee in later years claimed that he (Lee) wrote the suffrage bill, persuaded Bright to introduce it, and steered it through the house after Bright had won the council's approval. Circumstantial evidence supports his claim.

The bill passed the council, 6–2, then met stiffer opposition in the house, where Ben Sheeks, a young bachelor lawyer from South Pass City, led the attack. The press did not cover the debate, and the official record is disappointingly brief. It may be assumed that Sheeks used some of the stock arguments that had wide currency in the late 1860s. Almost all of the legislators had come recently from the East and were familiar with assertions like these: woman's place is in the home; only bad and ignorant women will vote; politics is a dirty pool; women don't know enough about government; voting will diminish respect for women; it will unsex them; it is contrary to the Bible; if women vote contrary to their husbands, there will be conflict; if they vote as their husbands do, it will only double the vote without changing the result.

The published record of the session shows that Ben Sheeks moved to postpone consideration of the suffrage bill indefinitely and that he offered a series of amendments, among them one to substitute "all colored women and squaws" for "women." It was reported after the session that some legislators were won over by the suggestion that the governor, who was a Republican, would veto the bill, and that the Democratic legislators could have some fun with him before he returned the bill to them. Governor Campbell had not tipped his hand, and it was generally supposed that he was not a woman's rights sympathizer. Lee had to maneuver adroitly because he was a Republican dealing with all Democrats in the legislature, while for personal reasons his relations with the governor were somewhat strained. Yet he won in the house by a 7–4 vote.

Governor Campbell took four days to make up his mind. Two of the three justices of the territorial supreme court encouraged him to sign the bill, and so did a few prominent Cheyenne women. Mrs. Morton E. Post later told Susan B. Anthony that she and several friends met at her house, went in a body to the bachelor governor's residence and obtained his signature on the bill by threatening to stay until he had signed.[4] Campbell was not yet a suffragist but decided that an experiment was justified. Lee said later that the decision to sign caused some of the legislators to curse the governor because they had counted on his veto.

While much testimony from participants and other knowledgeable citizens of the 1870s makes it reasonable to think that the attract-population argument was most important, and that at least a few legislators thought they were playing a game with the governor, the justice argument must not be overlooked. The woman suffrage act was of a piece with several other laws adopted by the same legislature, laws which showed sympathy for the rights of women. Two laws, copied from the Colorado statutes with a few changes in wording, gave rights which were in advance of those in many states. One of these gave married women control of their separate property, permitted them to work in trade or business, and allowed them to control their own earnings. The other provided for equal treatment of husband and wife in the distribution of an intestate's property. A third protection, which was far from universal in 1869, was given to Wyoming wives by adoption of a provision that a mortgage on the family homestead would not be binding on the wife unless she had freely and voluntarily signed it.

Also, the legislature was in advance of the rest of the country in forbidding discrimination on account of sex in the pay of equally qualified school teachers. Possibly in this instance, as in the suffrage act, the legislators were making a special effort to

4. Ida H. Harper, *Life and Works of Susan B. Anthony,* 3 vols. (Indianapolis: n.p., 1898–1908), 1:387.

attract women. And, since the 1870 U.S. Census showed only 305 school children and fifteen teachers (eight women and seven men), the commitment to equal pay did not require great sacrifices by the taxpayers. Yet, taken all together, the woman's rights laws adopted by the first legislature put it well ahead of its time.

Cheyenne's leading newspaper suggested that protections for married women were more important in a new territory than in settled states because the territory had more speculations, gambling, and dissipations. Married men sometimes supported such legislation out of concern for their daughters. About one-half of the members of the first legislature were married.

One can detect the handiwork of Lee in much of the woman's rights legislation. One of his responsibilities as secretary of the territory was to provide tools the legislators needed, which included sources and reference works. How fortunate it was for the woman's rights cause that the secretary of Wyoming in 1869 was an ardent suffragist. Not only were the legislators inexperienced, but their constituents, as well, had only recently been thrown together. They had no consensus, no cake of custom and tradition that had to be broken before innovative steps could be taken. Nor was there much southern influence in the territory to inhibit extension of rights to women. The flow of southerners to the Rocky Mountain West during the Civil War passed through or around Wyoming. Most of the people who came to Wyoming in the late 1860s had been born in New York, Pennsylvania, Ohio, Indiana, Illinois, and Missouri—states more or less directly east of Wyoming. Three-eighths of the 1870 population, however, were foreign-born, with Ireland, Germany, and England being the leading sources. Biographies can be found for only eight of the thirteen legislators who voted for woman suffrage. Two were natives of Virginia, the others of New York, Ohio, Iowa, Kentucky, Prussia, and Ireland.

Although the publicity given Wyoming for its suffrage leadership would in time pile up phenomenally, it began more slowly than expected. The first press notices were brief, even in Susan B. Anthony's suffrage newspaper, the *Revolution*. The eastern press had no correspondents in Cheyenne with pencils poised to dash off in-depth stories about what had happened. Disbelief, skepticism, and a "what's-going-on-here" tone characterized some of the reports. Editors were inclined to dismiss as inconsequential a bill passed by a small legislature in wild western territory where there were very few women. It wasn't that the editors knew nothing about Wyoming. In the past three years their newspapers had published many stories about Wyoming's railroad construction, end-of-track towns, prostitutes, vigilantes, alkali, and sagebrush.

Meetings of suffragists in the East buzzed with curiosity and excitement. They complimented Wyoming on its enlightenment. Susan B. Anthony urged women to emigrate to Wyoming, make a model state out of it, and send a woman to the U.S. Senate. She would go herself, she said, if she did not already have commitments to lead the reform movement in the East. Miss Anthony probably lost the last of this enthusiasm in January 1872 when she spent almost a week snowbound on a train in Wyoming. Other suffragists took up the "go-to-Wyoming" theme. Mutual aid societies were suggested. Before anything could be done, the critics rushed in, crying "let the New England spinsters go out there." The *New York Observer* said "Go, dear sisters, go, and 'stand not on the order of your going,' but go at once." [5] As a favorite reply to such insults, suffragists said that they were entitled to equality where they were, and they were going to continue to fight for their rights at home.

The flurry of short press notices reporting the adoption of the woman suffrage act was followed a few months later by two other flurries. As secretary, Lee became acting governor whenever the governor left the territory. When Governor Campbell was back East in February 1870, Lee with special assistance from one of the supreme court judges, John W. Kingman, struck another blow for the suffrage cause. He appointed three women to fill justice of the peace vacancies. As it turned out, only one qualified and served. This was Esther Morris of South

5. *Woman's Journal* 1 (January 22, 1870): 20.

Pass City, the 57-year-old wife of a poor provider who divided his time between mining and running a saloon in the village of 460 people.

The "first woman judge" was a colorful figure whose activities inspired longer stories than the spare announcements that had followed the passage of the woman suffrage bill. Since ultimately she would be proclaimed Wyoming's outstanding deceased citizen by the Wyoming Legislature in 1955 and would have her bronze statute placed in Statuary Hall, Washington, D.C., with a replica placed in front of the capitol in Cheyenne, a few paragraphs must be allotted to her here.

Almost six feet tall and weighing upwards of 180 pounds, the nation's first woman judge was called "mannish" by contemporaries, although a close friend, Prof. Grace Raymond Hebard of the University of Wyoming, said she was not as mannish as she looked. She was outspoken and blunt in conversation, though in no sense a militant suffragist or forerunner of the suffragettes. Born and brought up in New York State, she probably ended her formal schooling when she was orphaned at age eleven. She worked as a milliner until she was 28, when she married a civil engineer named Artemus Slack. He died soon thereafter, leaving her with an infant son. She and her son migrated to Peru, Illinois, where in 1845 she married a merchant, John Morris, a Polish immigrant, by whom she bore twin sons in 1852. The Illinois census of 1850 listed John Morris as a merchant with real estate worth $2,000, and in 1860 as "without business" and with no property, although his wife had real estate valued at $4,000 and personal property, $1,000. Like the "father of woman suffrage," William H. Bright, John Morris and his stepson, Edward A. Slack, migrated to South Pass City in 1868. Also like Bright, John Morris became a saloonkeeper. Esther Morris and the twins joined the rest of the family in June 1869. Many people believe that Esther Morris persuaded Bright to introduce his bill. Probably, however, she did not meet him until *after* the woman suffrage bill had become law. In a letter, which he wrote two weeks after the 1869 legislature had adjourned, Esther Morris's 18-year-old son Robert reported that he and his mother had called on Bright just after he had returned from the legislature to congratulate him on his success. Robert Morris wrote that when he was congratulated Bright "expressed himself pleased that there were some persons here who endorsed his views on woman suffrage," which is not what he would have said had he known Esther Morris's views before the visit, and had he been persuaded by her to introduce the bill.[6]

Justice Morris's term of eight and one-half months ended in November 1870. Her docket book, preserved in the Wyoming State Archives, Cheyenne, shows that she handled only twenty-six cases, twelve criminal and fourteen civil, involving mainly assault and battery or the collection of small debts. Her clerk was her son Robert, who kept a neat record. He was not overworked since South Pass City was a dying town. Its official population of 460 in 1870 was less than half of what it had been a year earlier.

Esther Morris was just getting accustomed to court routine when her term ended. She wanted to continue, but no political party would nominate her; so she could not be elected.

In June 1871, seven months after she had left the bench, Esther Morris swore out a warrant for her husband's arrest on grounds of assault and battery. The warrant was not served and the difficulty was settled out of court. Whoever filed a story on this incident garbled the details. It was reported from coast to coast that Justice Morris had sentenced her husband to jail for drunkenness. One editor warned that this affair illustrated the dangers inherent in woman suffrage. In fact, Esther Morris could not have sentenced her husband, had she wanted to, because she was out of office at the time.

Even more publicity than that involving Esther Morris resulted when women were summoned to serve on grand and petit juries in 1870 and 1871 in Laramie and Cheyenne. The *New York Times* reported the innovation on its front page and said editorially that there was much to be said both for and against feminine juries. The *New York Tribune* thought that female juries were "indecorous and not suitable." One reporter coined

6. *Revolution* 5 (January 13, 1870): 21.

a couplet: "Baby, baby, don't get in a fury,/Your mama's gone to sit on the jury." Another scribe related that the twelve members of a mixed jury (eight men and four women) spent a night together, locked up by the bailiff in one hotel room. Another story said that they spent four nights together. The district judge felt compelled to issue a denial in which he explained that the jury was on duty during only two nights, and that the women spent them in separate rooms, guarded by their own female bailiff. The *Woman's Journal* protested the spate of libelous falsehoods.

The evidence warrants the conclusion that the women were conscientious and effective jurors. They took their work more seriously than the men had done previously in the territory. Some of the male jurors had been known to spend more time relaxing over whiskey and cards than pondering the guilt or innocence of the accused. The female jurors believed that a law for Sunday closing of saloons should be enforced, and they saw to it that it was, until the next legislature repealed the law. In a day when many men in the West carried sidearms and when men accused of murder regularly pleaded self-defense, the women were less ready than men to accept such pleas without substantial supporting evidence.

People who did not want aggressive law enforcement objected to having female jurors. They pointed to the added expense of having two bailiffs and two or more hotel rooms. They said also that continued service of women on juries would disrupt the home. When a female juror in Cheyenne interrupted a murder trial by becoming sick, it was suggested that this could be expected to happen as long as women were called to jury service. The use of women on Wyoming juries ended in 1871 after new judges decreed that jury duty was not a necessary adjunct of suffrage. Women were not summoned again until 1950, except in a few cases when women were to be tried. During the many years when women were rarely summoned, very few people, men or women, complained. The men were willing to bear the burden, and the women permitted them to do so.

Intelligent observers of the female juries of 1870 and 1871 were laudatory. Chief Justice J. H. Howe, for example, praised

WYOMING

A photographer's essay by Bob Peterson

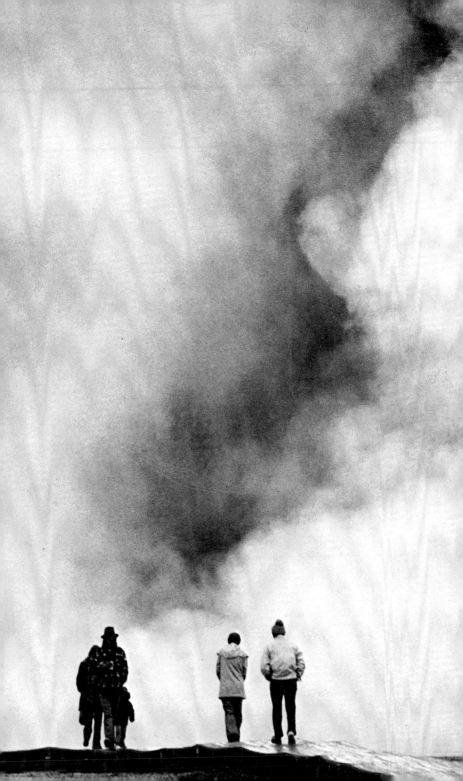

Photographs in sequence

Horses between Laramie and Centennial.
Teton Mountains.
Rock climbers in Medicine Bow National Forest.
Horseback riders, Yellowstone National Park.
Power lines near Cheyenne.
Sheep drive near Hanna.
Girl on horse near Hanna.
Geyser, Yellowstone National Park.
Storm in western Wyoming.
Herding cattle near Cheyenne.
Trucks at Cheyenne.
Houses in Laramie.
State capitol, Cheyenne.
Union Pacific Railroad train near Cheyenne.
Power lines along Route 130 near Centennial.
Antelope along Route 187.

the women who had served in his court: "With all my prejudices against the policy, I am under conscientious obligations to
say that these women acquitted themselves with such dignity,
decorum, propriety of conduct, and intelligence as to win the
admiration of every fair-minded citizen of Wyoming . . . the
experiment was a success." [7] Judge Howe added that he had
never had "any more faithful, intelligent and resolutely honest"
juries in eighteen years on the bench. This widely disseminated
testimonial was an excellent one to have on the record later
whenever the possibility of summoning women to jury duty
came up for discussion in Wyoming and elsewhere.

The one thousand voting-age women of Wyoming finally got
their first chance to cast ballots on September 2, 1870. After the
excitement associated with the activities of Justice Morris and
the female jurors, going to the polls seemed almost anticlimac-
tic. Most of the women voted, and thus proved wrong the skep-
tics who had predicted that they would not vote because they
had not asked for the privilege.

The women were given credit for the improved atmosphere
around the polling places in the 1870s. All was orderly and
peaceful, where in the elections of 1868 and 1869 there had
been drunkenness, fist fights, and even bloodshed. Male voters
had the courtesy to take their rowdyism elsewhere when women
came to the polls. Perhaps, however, the change can be at-
tributed in part to the fact that so many of the obstreperous transients had left the territory.

Since the secret ballot was not introduced in Wyoming until
1890, poll watchers could tell how the women voted by the
color or size of the ballots they selected. Most observers agreed
that the women voted Republican two-to-one in 1870 and that
they were instrumental in replacing a Democratic delegate to
Congress by a Republican. Inasmuch as a Democratic legislature had given them the ballot in 1869, Democrats in the next
(1871) legislature agreed that the women were ingrates who
should be punished. They had enough members to pass a repeal
measure in both houses and to override the governor's veto in

7. *Woman's Journal* 1 (April 23, 1870): 123.

the lower house, but they failed by one vote to override in the upper house. Gov. John A. Campbell, who had wavered in 1869, had become a suffragist in 1871. The unsuccessful repeal effort was reported on the front page of the *New York Times*.

Two Republicans, one Democrat, and one Populist in the council voted to sustain the governor's veto. Had anyone of the four voted the other way, the veto would have been overridden and the suffrage experiment would have ended. The pressure on the governor and the four council members who supported him was heavy. The territory's leading Republican newspaper joined the Democrats in calling for repeal, alleging that woman suffrage was "repugnant to the wishes of a majority of refined and intelligent women and her direct participation is unchaste and subversive of the natural order of things." [8] Only "the suffrage shriekers, the unsexed and uncultivated . . . of the Territory," favored woman suffrage, the editor insisted. Governor Campbell noted in his diary that he was offered $2,000 and other benefits if he would sign the repeal bill. It may be assumed that the friends of suffrage in the council also received bribe offers.

Four of the seven men who had been or would be elected to represent the territory as delegates to Congress were members of the nine-man council which divided five-to-four on the repeal question. They were S. F. Nuckolls and W. R. Steele, rough-hewn Democrats who favored repeal, and W. W. Corlett and S. W. Downey, polished Republican lawyers who opposed. Had oratory been influential, it would have been no contest, because Corlett and Downey excelled in that art. Steele was quoted as having said in the council debate: "The Governor hadn't got no right to veto the bill. . . . Politics is a very dirty pool. . . . No woman aint got no right to set on a jury unless she is a man." [9] On the other hand, Downey argued that female suffrage, more than anything else, had already given "positiveness to the reputation and character of Wyoming" and therefore the experiment should not be cut off in its infancy without a fair trial. He said, further:

8. *Cheyenne Leader,* November 21, 1871. The quotation which follows is taken from the same paper, December 11, 1871.

9. *Laramie Daily Sentinel,* December 6, 1871.

we find the Democratic party endeavoring to impede the progress of this mighty reform. But all their efforts to suppress its advancement will be as vain and futile as were those of the old Danish King Canute, who endeavored to make the ocean waves obey his mandate, and although this great reform may today, so far as actual results are concerned, appear as insignificant as a flake of snow, fresh driven from the frosty clouds on high, it will speedily roll and revolve itself into an avalanche that will annihilate and sweep away all opposition.[10]

It is sometimes suggested that stable, conservative married men gave women in western territories the right to vote in order to bolster their political power against threats from transient bachelors. This theory is not supported by the Wyoming experience. About one-half of the 1869 legislators were bachelors (the status of a few is unknown), and bachelors were no less ready to support woman suffrage than the married men were. More than three-fourths (17/22) of the members of the 1871 legislature were bachelors, and they were found on both sides of the question. Four of the five married men, two in each house, favored repeal. The vote of the one married man who opposed repeal was essential to sustain the veto, but so also were several votes of bachelors. Governor Campbell, who vetoed the repeal bill, was a bachelor who was about to get married. The four men who blocked repeal in the council included three bachelors, two of whom would get married during the following year.

After the suffrage experiment narrowly missed extinction in 1871, it had no more close calls. Many people who had been opposed or indifferent became advocates. A repeal bill was introduced in 1875, but got nowhere. Every governor of the territory praised woman suffrage thereafter and no legislator thought it worth his while to introduce another repeal bill.

How many people migrated to Wyoming because of the woman suffrage act and the publicity that followed it, is speculative. It could not have been many; no one ever publicly gave that as a reason for coming. The U.S. Census taken in June 1870, six months after passage of the suffrage bill, it is true, did show about 1,100 more people than the special census of June

10. *Woman's Journal* 2 (December 9, 1871): 388.

1869, but the special census was probably incomplete. Certainly the preponderance of males continued. The 1870 census reported six men over 21 for every woman over 21; and only 243 single women over 21, including widowed grandmothers. When a Wyoming bachelor married, it was usually to some eastern girl he had known before he went West.

A few hundred women found jobs as domestic servants, prostitutes, teachers, laundresses, tailoresses, seamstresses, milliners, dressmakers, and restaurant employees. Some easterners suggested that single women should file on free land available under the Homestead Act of 1862. A female correspondent who spent several days in Cheyenne at election time in 1870 helped squelch that suggestion with a warning published in the *Woman's Journal*. She reported that although woman suffrage was definitely a success, the eastern and southern parts of the territory were "almost one unbroken, arid desert." [11] A few men filed on homesteads beginning in 1870, but not one woman did so before 1875, when two filed in Laramie County.

Westbound emigrants who were smart enough to investigate job opportunities tended to avoid Wyoming. The Union Pacific paid low wages to its coal miners and section hands, and were quick to bring in Chinese when whites asked for more pay. Mineral resources other than coal could not be marketed at a profit. The territory survived one crisis when Congress chose to disregard President Grant's recommendation that the territory be abolished and its parts distributed to the surrounding territories. Grant thought Wyoming's small population and dubious growth prospects did not warrant its continuation. Residents of southeastern Wyoming divided on the issue, some favoring abolishment because their area would have been added to Colorado and they would soon have had the advantages of statehood. Suffragists opposed because they would have to fight for their rights all over again in Colorado. The matter was dropped in 1874.

As previously, many single men came and went in the 1870s. A comparison of the manuscript censuses of 1870 and 1880

11. *Woman's Journal* 1 (October 8, 1870): 320.

reveals that only one male in thirteen of the ones in Wyoming in 1870 was still resident in 1880. Many of the women cannot be traced because they changed their names, but probably transiency characterized them too. Transient or not, Wyoming's pioneer women almost without exception were unaggressive. They enjoyed little leisure and had had no training or experience in leadership. Esther Morris illustrated the prevailing attitude when she advised other women to have confidence in the good will of the men and not to pester them. Her appointment as "first woman judge" thrust her into the limelight at age fifty-seven for the first time in her life, and made her the best-known woman in the territory. With a better education and with speaking or writing skills she might have become a leader, although her age was against her, and she had not been an activist before coming to Wyoming. Poverty handicapped her. The fees she collected as justice of the peace, listed in her docket book, totaled only $135.70.

Esther Morris left her husband in 1873 to live close to her sons in Laramie and Cheyenne. In the 1870s they could provide her with little more than board and room. Had she been able to attend the National Woman Suffrage Association's convention in Washington, D.C., in January 1871, just two months after her retirement from the bench, she would have received a great ovation. Intead, she sent a letter, which was read and applauded at the convention:

> So far as woman suffrage has progressed in this Territory we are entirely indebted to men. . . . I feel that my work . . . [as justice of the peace] has been satisfactory, although I have often regretted that I was not better qualified. . . . While enjoying the franchise we have not been sufficiently educated up to it . . . [but] I now think that we shall be able to sustain the position granted to us.[12]

A year later, she attended a suffrage convention in San Francisco and said a few words about her experiences but did not try to deliver an address.

In Laramie, where Esther Morris lived a few years while her

12. *Laramie Daily Sentinel,* January 21, 1871.

oldest son edited a weekly newspaper there, women in August 1873 tried to get her to run for the legislature. She agreed to run, then two weeks later withdrew. Perhaps she realized that the men of Wyoming were not yet ready to send a woman to the legislature. Only two women ran for the legislature in the territorial period. One received five votes, the other received eight, when several hundred were needed for election.

Since Esther Morris said little in public and wrote nothing for publication except the letter quoted above, she contributed almost nothing to the woman's rights movement after her brief tenure as justice of the peace. She did attend a second national meeting, the one in Philadelphia in 1876. The *History of Woman Suffrage* records that at that meeting "Judge Esther Morris, of Wyoming, said a few words in regard to suffrage in that territory." [13]

The selection of Esther Morris in 1955 as Wyoming's outstanding deceased citizen can be understood only in light of the fact that almost all school children of the state in the 1920s and 1930s were taught that she was the "Mother of Woman Suffrage." They accepted the story that Bright introduced the woman suffrage bill in 1869 because he had promised Esther Morris at a tea party in her home prior to his election that he would do so. Prof. Grace Raymond Hebard, librarian and professor of political economy at the University of Wyoming, propagated the tea party story assiduously until she died in 1936. Even though the tea party is apocryphal and Esther Morris's influence on Bright is questionable, her selection as Wyoming's outstanding deceased citizen is not without merit. She is representative of many nineteenth-century women of ability who were denied opportunity for fulfillment.

The woman who, next to Esther Morris, won recognition for suffrage activity in Wyoming was Mrs. M. E. (Amalia) Post, a Cheyenne woman whose husband was a delegate to Congress. More than any other woman in Wyoming, Amalia Post worked

13. Elizabeth Cady Stanton, Susan B. Anthony et al, eds., *History of Woman Suffrage,* 6 vols. (Rochester and New York: privately published about 1887), 3:35.

for woman suffrage in 1869 and 1871. Located in Cheyenne, she was conveniently close to the action. She begged Governor Campbell to sign the woman suffrage bill in 1869, and she gave similar attention in 1871 to the doubtful member of the quartet which finally sustained the governor's veto of repeal. Like Esther Morris, she spoke and wrote very little and attended few national suffrage conventions. In the years when the National Woman Suffrage Association listed one woman from each territory or state as an association vice-president, Esther Morris was so honored in 1876 and Amalia Post, for twenty years, beginning in 1880. Both were Republicans with Democratic husbands.

A third woman, Therese A. Jenkins, emerged as a leader in the late 1880s. A young Cheyenne wife, she took charge of the state WCTU's franchise work and served in 1891 as national superintendent of that organization's suffrage promotion. Unlike Esther Morris and Amalia Post, she had public speaking ability. She was the only Wyoming woman who participated to any extent in suffrage campaigns outside of Wyoming, working in Colorado, for example, in 1893, and, according to her own account, speaking in thirteen other states. When someone told her that chivalry would always protect a woman, she replied ''Well, yes, maybe; but it is well to have a broom or a weapon around, for fear 'chivalry' may not get there.'' [14]

Wyoming women learned early that they should not take seriously the equal pay commitment made by the first legislature and the right to hold office which was included with the right to vote in the woman suffrage act. Female teachers regularly received less pay than their male counterparts, whom they outnumbered, and the few women who aspired to office in the 1870s were denied. Women had no significant part in party nominating conventions, and all but a few soon quit seeking office. In 1882, however, Mrs. Lizzie W. Smith broke the ice by winning election as county superintendent of schools in Carbon County; and gradually thereafter more county superintendencies were assigned to women. After twenty years of ''equality''

14. *Woman's Journal* 22 (April 4, 1891): 106.

three women sought election to the constitutional convention which had been called in 1889 to prepare for statehood; but only men were elected to the fifty-five convention seats.

During its territorial years, 1869–1890, Wyoming was a unique showcase, laboratory, and experiment station for the national woman suffrage movement. Utah Territory's experiment, 1870–1887, was terminated by act of Congress; and Washington Territory's experiment, 1883–1887, was ended by a decision of its supreme court. As the first and most enduring experiment exhibit, Wyoming's received much attention nationally. Just as men had been responsible for the introduction of woman suffrage in Wyoming, so men assumed most of the burden of praising and defending their handiwork. Although Wyoming's most exuberant suffragist, Edward M. Lee, left the territory in 1871 to practice law in New York City, he often lectured for pay in New England states in the next ten years. In 1871 he wrote an editorial in the *Wyoming Tribune* (Cheyenne) praising the experiment excessively: "Wyoming has given the woman movement an impetus, ten thousand times greater than that received by its theoretical discussion during a decade of years before Eastern lyceums. Others have talked; we have acted. . . ." [15] Apparently Lee expected the experiment to advance faster than it did. In particular, he wanted women in the legislature immediately, instead of waiting forty-two years for that small step forward.

Several territorial officials spent their own money on lecture tours in various states, notably Supreme Court Justice John W. Kingman and Gov. John W. Hoyt. Kingman, a Harvard graduate, practiced law in Laramie after he left the bench in 1873. He presented a balanced and comprehensive statement before a Massachusetts legislative committee in 1876. He said that women had gradually increased their participation in voting until nearly all of them were going to the polls. He conceded that few women attended party caucuses or ran for public office. In 1882 Kingman devoted two weeks to lecturing in the Nebraska suffrage campaign.

15. *Woman's Journal* 2 (August 26, 1871): 368.

Governor Hoyt (1878–1882) was an eloquent public speaker who had been an ardent suffragist since youth. Before coming to Wyoming he had lived in Ohio and Wisconsin. The *Woman's Journal* regularly praised his work. Twenty thousand copies of a speech he had given in Philadelphia in 1882 were distributed in Pennsylvania alone by the National Woman Suffrage Association.

Gov. Francis E. Warren and Delegate to Congress Joseph M. Carey did not go far out of their way to lecture, but they stood ready to answer questions and to parry thrusts from anti-suffragists. Warren in his two terms as territorial governor wrote many letters in reply to threadbare questions which required little more than a yes or no answer. For example, a Kansas woman asked him in 1886 if a majority of women voted, if family harmony was destroyed when a woman voted in opposition to her husband, if women were treated respectfully at the polls, if the presence of women at the polls exercised a refining influence, whether the law required women to pay poll tax, whether women supported the most moral candidates, regardless of party, and what offices women had served in satisfactorily. Also in 1886, a Saint Louis woman who said she was writing an article on the subject asked how long the women had had the vote, what class of women voted, what influence they had on politics, whether their presence at the polls affected the conduct of male voters, if any woman had ever been known to accept a bribe, if judges compelled women to serve in juries, what provision was made at night for mixed juries, what offices women held, whether the best citizens approved, and whether intelligent, upper-class women voted at all elections.

Mrs. William H. Bright, whom many people credited with having induced her husband to introduce the suffrage bill, and Bright himself participated to a limited extent in the Colorado suffrage campaign of 1876–1877 when they lived in Denver.

Laramie and Cheyenne editors generally praised the results of woman suffrage. James H. Hayford, editor of the *Laramie Sentinel,* whose editorials were often quoted in the *Woman's Journal,* usually maintained that woman suffrage had been a complete success. He was not always consistent, saying sometimes that women "frequently" voted contrary to their husbands, without making them angry, and at other times, that wives nearly always voted as their husbands did. The best argument for woman suffrage, he said, was that "it doubles the power and influence of the home element (always the best element) in the government of the country." [16] Sometimes he admitted that woman suffrage had not reduced the amount of intemperance, gambling, and prostitution, and explained that women constituted such a small percentage of the population that they had little political power and influence. Thus Hayford touched on a fact that not only severely limited the political power of the women but also kept them from becoming offensive to male politicians and saloonkeepers. At the end of the territorial period in 1890 the ratio of voting-age men to women was about three to one. The women, Hayford conceded, had been unable materially to "purify the ballot box" and to keep bad men out of elective offices. As a result, he concluded, "while few people charge it [woman suffrage] with any evil results, a great many don't credit it with any beneficial influence, and quite a large portion regard it with indifference." [17] Hayford seems to have been the one who originated the challenge, thrown out repeatedly by himself and others, to opponents "to find two persons in all Wyoming Territory who will assert over their own names and addresses, that woman suffrage has had any bad results." [18]

The National Woman Suffrage Association gathered up batches of testimonials offered by Wyoming governors, judges, editors, and ministers of the gospel and published them from time to time in "tracts" for distribution in many states and territories. Hundreds of thousands of leaflets were issued with titles such as "Woman Suffrage in Wyoming," "Wyoming Speaks for Herself," and "Falsehoods about Wyoming."

16. *Woman's Journal* 29 (November 19, 1898): 376.

17. *Woman's Journal* 20 (July 13, 1889): 220, and *Laramie Weekly Sentinel,* June 22, 1889.

18. "Woman Suffrage in Wyoming," a leaflet, May 1, 1889, published by the American Woman Suffrage Association, Boston. A copy is preserved in the Sophie Smith Research Room, Smith College.

All kinds of visitors stopped in Wyoming from Susan B. Anthony, who called the territory "the home of the brave and the land of the free," in 1871, to J. H. Beadle, who reported several years later in his book, *Western Wilds and the Men Who Redeem Them* (1877 edition), that one-fifth (300) of the women in Wyoming were prostitutes and that there were 100 saloons. He said, for example, that Cheyenne had thirty-five saloons and forty-five prostitutes; Laramie, twenty-six saloons and twenty-five prostitutes. These figures were probably a little high. Some of the visitors made searching inquiries, interviewing prominent men and women; others based their reports on little more than what they saw from train windows.

Consistent with their meekness and low profile, women of the territory kept their grievances to themselves. An exception was a Rawlins tailor's wife who wrote a letter which was read in the Massachusetts legislature in 1884 and may have helped defeat a suffrage bill. She said that Wyoming men controlled the votes of their wives and daughters, that friendships ended when a woman failed to vote for a friend's husband, that women dreaded election time, that women had no voice in the selection of candidates, and that they did not know enough about government to vote intelligently. Antisuffragists in the East capitalized on these charges, while friends of suffrage summoned Wyoming's stalwarts to the barricades. Editor Hayford responded with the assertion that this was the first letter he had ever heard of from a Wyoming woman against suffrage. The charges were not true for Laramie, he said, and he would let Rawlins people refute them. The editor of the *Rawlins Journal* answered only indirectly when he declared that four people out of five would vote for continuation of woman suffrage if given a chance, and that among the best people forty-nine out of fifty were favorable. Lizzie W. Smith, county superintendent of schools in Rawlins, and one of the few women of Wyoming whose testimonials ever appeared in print, added her opinion that all women in Wyoming would vote against a candidate whose character was not "correct."

Women who were expected to vote only for men whose conduct was correct, were expected also to be correct in their own conduct. Following a dance at a ranch seven miles west of Cheyenne in October 1887, an ungallant young man appeared before the school board and charged that a school teacher had absented herself from the dance with her partner for two periods totaling four hours. The teacher, who was described as "handsome," and her friend were able to account for their actions satisfactorily and the school board dismissed the immoral conduct charges. The propriety of the teacher's dancing seems not to have been questioned in this case. Only a few churches frowned on dancing.

The overwhelming majority of men in Wyoming in the 1880s found nothing objectionable in the political behavior of the women. They were pleased to note the absence of agitation. When praising female behavior in politics the men almost always recited that they had improved the atmosphere around the polls, and had raised the level of morality among male candidates because both parties knew that immoral candidates would be rejected by the women, and concluded with the ultimate accolade, "they are not office seekers."

It seems likely that most of the men would not have gone out of their way to initiate woman suffrage if they had it to do over again, but by the same token they saw no reason for doing away with woman suffrage, unless some kind of emergency arose. What appeared to be such an emergency arose in 1889. When Gov. Francis E. Warren announced plans for a constitutional convention, Amalia Post and a few friends called a convention of Cheyenne women to discuss their representation in the constitutional convention and protection of their rights. With Amalia Post presiding, the 100 women present voted respectfully to ask favorable consideration of a resolution, "That we demand of the constitutional convention that woman suffrage be affirmed in the state constitution." The women's convention took no position with respect to representation, although Amalia Post said she trusted that women would have fair representation. Her trust was misplaced, since no woman was elected, although three in Laramie were candidates.

The threat to equality in 1889 lay in the fact that most men and not a few women almost certainly would have given up woman suffrage if it had come to a choice between that and statehood. Five territories—North and South Dakota, Montana, Washington, and Idaho—were preparing to seek statehood just ahead of Wyoming. Each of the five had more people than Wyoming, and a better claim to recognition. All five in their constitutional conventions rejected proposals that woman suffrage be included in their constitutions. In all, one of the factors contributing to defeat was fear that the U.S. Congress would not admit a state with woman suffrage in its constitution. Since no state represented in Congress had woman suffrage it was assumed that strong objections would be raised.

In Wyoming's constitutional convention, which met in September 1889, a Cheyenne lawyer proposed that woman suffrage be submitted to the electors as a separate article. He pointed out that the electors had never had an opportunity to vote on woman suffrage. He and some petitioners whom he represented were afraid that either the electors would reject the constitution with woman suffrage in it, or the Congress would. In the debate that followed, two members of the convention advocated staying out of the Union forever rather than give up woman suffrage. The proposal for a separate vote lost by a vote of 20–8 in committee of the whole. Thus the constitution with woman suffrage in it was submitted to the electors in November 1889 and received their approval by a majority of three to one.

As expected, strong opposition developed in the U.S. House of Representatives. A member from Georgia argued that suffrage was intended for men, not women and children. Another member from Atlanta said he had learned that women in Wyoming bought and sold votes. Other objections came from Tennessee, New Jersey, and Illinois. Most of the debate centered on woman suffrage, although questions were asked also about the sufficiency of the territory's population. After two damaging amendments were defeated, each by only six votes, the House passed the statehood bill, 139–127, with sixty-three members not voting. The Senate later approved, 29–18, after listening to complaints about small population and woman suffrage, and President Benjamin Harrison signed the bill on July 10, 1890.

Wyoming had sought statehood at just the right time. As a

result of victories in 1888, one party had control of Congress and the presidency for the first time since 1876. Even more important for Wyoming, it was the Republican party. During most of the territorial period there were a few more Democrats than Republicans in Wyoming, but in 1888 Republicans won most of the legislative seats and re-elected Joseph M. Carey delegate to Congress. Also, two-thirds of the men elected to the "nonpartisan" constitutional convention in 1889 were Republicans. GOP congressmen could feel reasonably confident that Wyoming would become a Republican state. Wyoming was fortunate also that the Republican party was more sympathetic to woman suffrage than the Democrats were. Had there been Democratic control of Congress in 1890, almost certainly Wyoming would have had to give up either woman suffrage or statehood. Given a choice, the Wyoming electors probably would have taken statehood. It seems likely, however, that with Democrats in control of Congress, statehood would have been postponed, since the thought of adding another Republican state would have been abhorrent.

The friendly majority in Congress made it possible for Joseph M. Carey, Wyoming's Republican delegate, to declare flatly and confidently, without contradiction, that the territory had between 110,000 and 125,000 people. Certainly Carey knew better, but he knew also that no official count had been made since 1880. Soon after statehood, the 1890 census reports would be released and would show the population to be only 62,555. The problem that had plagued Wyoming since earliest times—how to attract settlers to its semiarid land and high altitude—was still present.

Wyoming's progress toward statehood was watched closely by the two national suffrage associations, the American and the National, which merged in 1890 to form the National American Woman Suffrage Association (NAWSA). When the Wyoming constitutional convention approved woman suffrage, the *Woman's Journal* said "This is the greatest event that has occurred in American history since the Declaration of Independence and the adoption of the Federal Constitution. . . . It es-

tablishes for the first time in history a true Republic." [19]
Similar expressions followed the achievement of statehood on
July 10, 1890. At Wyoming's statehood celebration, Therese A.
Jenkins gave one of the two major addresses.

In 1891 the call for the 33rd annual national suffrage convention proclaimed "Wyoming, all hail; the first true republic the
world has ever seen." [20] The suffragists stepped up their activity thereafter with the result that Colorado became the second
suffrage state in 1893, Utah the third in 1896, and Idaho the
fourth, later in 1896.

The Wyoming House of Representatives aided the suffrage
crusade by adopting the following in 1893:

> Resolved that the possession and exercise of suffrage by women in
> Wyoming . . . has wrought no harm and has done great good in
> many ways; that it has largely aided in banishing crime, pauperism,
> and vice from this State . . . has secured peaceful and orderly
> elections, good government, and a remarkable degree of civilization
> and public order . . . not one county in Wyoming has a poor-house
> . . . our jails are all empty, and crime, except that committed by
> strangers in the State, is almost unknown . . . we urge every
> civilized community on earth to enfranchise its women without
> delay . . . we request the press throughout the civilized world to
> call attention of their readers to these resolutions. [21]

Although many newspapers published stories about the legislative body's action, the resolution cannot be found in the Session
Laws or Journal of the House for 1893. However, the House
Journal does include a note from twenty-two Cheyenne women,
thanking the legislators "for passing the resolutions favoring
universal suffrage, so complimentary to the women of the
State." This entry in the House Journal must refer to the resolution quoted above. Of course, crime and pauperism had not
been banished from the state. Yet the details listed were not en-

19. *Woman's Journal* 20 (September 28, 1889): 305.

20. Susan B. Anthony and Ida Husted Harper, eds., *History of Woman Suffrage*, 4:176.

21. The full text of the resolution appears in *Woman's Journal* 25 (August 18, 1894): 338.

tirely fictitious. The 1890 census had just been published, and one of the items included was the number of paupers in almshouses. Wyoming was listed as having no almshouses. All other states and territories had at least one. In Wyoming's small population the counties distributed small sums to the poor without collecting them in almshouses. That the jails were all empty is quite as questionable as the suggestion that woman suffrage deserved credit for their being empty.

"Equal Rights" appeared on the state seal. "Equality State" became first the unofficial and later the official nickname. Wyoming was the first state to elect a woman to state office—Estelle Reel, state superintendent of public instruction in 1894. Wyoming shares with Texas priority in electing a woman governor; both elected women to head their state governments in 1924.

Mrs. Nellie Tayloe Ross's election illustrates the penchant of political leaders to capitalize on the popularity of a man who dies in office by substituting his widow. Gov. William B. Ross, a Democrat, died suddenly on October 2, 1924, of complications following an appendectomy. He had served almost two years of the four-year term to which he had been elected in 1922. Under Wyoming law it was the responsibility of the voters to elect someone on November 4, 1924, to serve the remaining two years of the term. The two major parties held special conventions in mid-October to nominate their candidates. The Democrats chose Mrs. Ross; the Republicans nominated a Casper attorney and former speaker of the state house of representatives, Eugene J. Sullivan. While Sullivan campaigned during the three weeks available, Mrs. Ross stayed home, letting her friends campaign for her. She announced that she planned to continue her husband's programs and policies. She won handily, although the Republicans, as usual, won control of both houses of the legislature, and elected their candidates for the U.S. Senate and U.S. House of Representatives.

Without much question, considerations of charity, sympathy, and chivalry had prevailed in the election. Trained as a kindergarten teacher, Nellie Tayloe Ross had taught briefly before her marriage in 1902. Since that time she had been fully occupied with domestic duties and bringing up three sons. She had shown no interest in the woman's rights movement, which was probably an asset because Wyoming voters had given little encouragement to activitists or female "office seekers."

Gov. Nellie Tayloe Ross enjoyed the tutelage of Joseph C. O'Mahoney, Cheyenne attorney who would later become U.S. senator, and David J. Howell, holdover attorney general. Without them her first months in office would have been much more difficult. She had little influence in the Republican-controlled legislature and on state boards, on which she served with the other four elective state officeholders, all Republicans. With some plausibility Wyoming claimed that she was the nation's first woman governor because she was inaugurated before Gov. Miriam A. Ferguson of Texas, after both had been elected on the same day.

After two years of satisfactory performance in difficult circumstances, Mrs. Ross lost in a bid for re-election. By this time the emotional appeal associated with her election in 1924 had dissipated. Republican women who had been involved in the state's subdued promotion of woman's rights spoke out against her for the first time in 1926. Therese A. Jenkins, who had been identified with woman's rights since her address at the statehood celebration in 1890, wrote an "open letter" which was disseminated all over the state: "What has Mrs. Ross done to particularly deserve the votes of women? Has she ever, since coming to Wyoming, taken any interest in Woman's Suffrage? Has she ever been a delegate to a Woman's Suffrage Convention, to a WCTU meeting? . . . she was elected . . . purely on the basis of sympathy and charity. . . . Now, that issue is dead. . . ." [22] And so it was. Most of the Republicans who had voted for Mrs. Ross in 1924 voted for their own party's candidate in 1926.

Wyoming has made much of its having had the first woman governor and of its other claims to equality. Yet its long-term performance in the woman's rights movement has not been sensational. Colorado, Idaho, and Utah elected women to their

22. *Wyoming State Tribune and Cheyenne State Leader,* October 3, 1926.

state legislatures before Wyoming did. The Equality State waited until 1910 before electing a woman to its legislature and has never had more than seven women in its legislature at one time—below average for the states. It has never sent a woman to Congress. Not until 1915, after an urgent plea from Gov. John B. Kendrick, did the legislature give women custody of their children, as against their husbands; limit the husband's right to will away from his wife almost all of his property; and assure the wife a respectable homestead exemption.

In the 1960s and 1970s the federal government pushed the Equality State toward equality faster than many of its people wanted to go. The state's Commission on the Status of Women included in its 1972 report to the governor the statement that "Although our state is known as the 'Equality State' . . . sex discrimination does exist and, in many cases, is accepted as normal. . . . Employment opportunities for women are curtailed sharply by sexual discrimination." There was considerable resistance to the Equal Rights Amendment before it was ratified by a vote of 17–12 in the Wyoming Senate in 1973. The most influential ERA advocate was Thyra Thomson, third-term secretary of state. Mother of three sons, widow of Congressman Keith Thomson, who died at forty-one in December 1960, two months after his election to the U.S. Senate, Mrs. Thomson was first elected secretary of state in 1962. Her popularity and persuasive argument disarmed opponents of the ERA.

To understand the wide gap between promise and performance in the extension of rights to women, it must be remembered that Wyoming has been a man's world. With six times as many men as women over twenty-one in 1870 and three times as many in 1890, few people seriously considered having women share equally with men in political and economic affairs. As late as 1930 there were seven men over twenty-one for every five women. Most of the pioneers had a very limited perception of equality. It meant little more to them than the right to vote; thus they unwittingly erected a false front when they boasted about their equality.

Wyoming has not deviated from national norms in the promotion of democratic practices other than woman suffrage. Cautious conservatism has prevailed. Wyoming has preferred to let other states take the lead, as its constitutional convention did in 1889 when it copied nine-tenths of the new constitution from models borrowed from North Dakota, South Dakota, Montana, and Idaho. After there has been enough experimentation in other states, Wyoming may choose to follow.

Populism in the 1890s and progressivism a generation later caused relatively little stir. The initiative and referendum amendment submitted in 1912 was defeated mainly because many who went to the polls did not vote either way on the amendment. Such an amendment was finally adopted in 1968. No action, however, has been initiated or referred since 1968, partly because the preliminary requirements are burdensome. A petition must be signed by qualified voters equal to 15 percent of those who voted in the preceding general election and resident in at least two-thirds of the counties before the proposal is submitted to the people. Extraordinary measures to save money were considered in a special session of the legislature in December 1933, but all measures were rejected. Among the unacceptable proposals were a one-house legislature, election of the governor by the legislature, selection of a state administrator by the legislature, and reduction of the number of counties from twenty-three to six.

Racial, ethnic, and religious minorities in general have received treatment comparable to that accorded them in other WASP states, although the small percentages of minorities and their low profile have contributed to the mistaken notion that there is no discrimination. Racist overtones appeared in the "Black 14" incident at the University of Wyoming in 1969. Lloyd Eaton, the head football coach, without first consulting his administrative superiors, summarily dismissed from the football team fourteen black players who appeared in his office on a Thursday morning wearing black armbands. They asked for permission to wear the armbands in a home game to be played two days later with the Mormon school, Brigham Young University. The black players wanted to wear the armbands as a protest against alleged race discrimination practiced by the Church of Jesus Christ of the Latter-day Saints (Mormons). Coach Eaton denounced the wearing of the armbands as a breach of discipline because he had ordered members of his football squad not to engage in any demonstrations. The University of Wyoming Board of Trustees upheld Coach Eaton, although they restored to the blacks their pecuniary benefits for the remainder of the academic year.

The "Black 14" incident divided the faculty at the university and the people of the state. The football team, which had won its first three games in 1969, defeated Brigham Young without the black players but lost all of the other games that season. Football fans who were accustomed to victories suffered intensely during the next six lean years before success returned in 1976. When Bishop David R. Thornberry of the Wyoming Episcopal Diocese announced in 1976 his desire to retire, the *Casper Star-Tribune* published these comments which Bishop Thornberry had made in an interview: "The affair concerning the black athletes revealed deep racial prejudices in many places in Wyoming where it was unsuspected. People were as much incensed because they were black as they were because they broke the discipline . . . the people in Wyoming have as far to go as any people in eliminating their racial prejudice." [23] It was common knowledge that Bishop Thornberry's defense of the black athletes had divided his church and had brought much trouble to his administration.

The state's posture with respect to reform in general has been what might be expected from a sparsely populated, have-not state in which the need for hard work and frugality have discouraged deviant behavior. Theoretically lightning, which struck in the first legislature in 1869, could have struck again sometime before 1976 and inspired some other spectacular innovative reform, but it never did.

In retrospect, in the man's world of Wyoming Territory, the idea that votes for women would attract people proved to be invalid. It was more effective to let it be known that young men could find employment as cowboys. The cattlemen had very little to do with bringing woman suffrage to Wyoming. They

23. *Casper Star-Tribune*, June 21, 1976.

were not represented in the first legislature and rarely became enthusiastic about woman's rights, but they had much to do with building the economic base necessary for statehood. They could make something of the Great American Desert when others failed.

4

The Cowboy State

Wyoming—the purest cattle state of all.

—Mari Sandoz

IF Wyoming failed to attract women, it succeeded superbly in attracting that all-time masculine figure, the cowboy. Other states can rightly claim to share in the making of the cowboy myth; but Wyoming became the place where the script of the myth was written, and it enthusiastically adopted the image, imprinted it on its license plates, named its university athletic teams after it, and proudly continues to call itself "the cowboy state."

The country and the culture were primed to accept and cultivate the cowboy by the last half of the nineteenth century. Completion of the first transcontinental railroad in 1869 left Wyoming with a questionable economic base and a population of barely 9,000—less than one person for each ten square miles of land. There appeared to be little hope for significant development of any of the industries that flourished in some other western states and territories—crop farming, manufacturing, lumbering, fishing, and shipping. People in Wyoming thought mining and livestock offered more promise than anything else. But hopes regarding gold mining faded in 1869, and the pioneers had to depend for survival on coal mining, the railroad, and the federal government.

And livestock. Most of the territory consisted of rangeland. Bison herds had lived for centuries on this natural resource. But by the 1870s these grasseating beasts had been slaughtered to such an extent that vast stretches of prairie appeared to be almost untouched. Across the High Plains of eastern Wyoming grew vast seas of tall needlegrass and bluestem, and shorter buffalo grass, blue grama, bluegrass, June grass, and wheatgrass. Emigrants found these grasses short, dry, and sparse in comparison with those of the Middle West; but they discovered them also to be quite rich in livestock feed values. Even the half of the range dotted with sagebrush could support some livestock—sheep, if not cattle.

Historical and geographical conditions favored the emergence of the cowboy as an archetypical figure for the nation. The trappers had their propagandizers; but they never caught on as a universal type—one that both children and adults all over the country could have fantasies about and role play in one way or another. It remained for several good writers, some actors, and changes in the culture, particularly in urbanization and industrialization, to reconstruct the cowboy from his incomplete and primitive reality to a masculine image fleshed out in contemporary imagination.

After the Civil War the United States continued to industrialize and it did so on a vast scale. Now the great clothing mills of New England, and the steel mills of Pennsylvania, the coal and iron mines of North and South, the vast network of rails and telegraph and telephone—all combined to create a complex civilization in which the individual felt he counted for very little and where the daily routine became boring if not downright deadly. Even so, the majority of the population of the United States lived in rural areas throughout the nineteenth century. Both conditions tended to create a yearning for a romantic figure. It was hard to make a hero out of a farmer when too many people knew the drudgery of barn and field. Some distance was required to enhance the subject. Although the reasons for the appeal of the cowboy are not easily explained, the attempt of people to escape from a complex technological society appears to have encouraged the appeal of the Western stereotype.

Wyoming offered the ideal conditions for fostering cowboys in their real and fictional forms. Isolated and sparsely populated but fecund with grass and blessed with the open space needed for cattle raising, it was the place some people went, even a century ago, to get away from it all. One easterner who vacationed in Wyoming, and went back again and again, created one of the great cowboy stereotypes in the Virginian. After Owen Wister's book by that name was published in 1902, it went through fifteen printings its first year, and is still in print.[1] It was, above all, isolation the Virginian sought. Wister has his hero comment on the "lonesomeness" of Wyoming: " 'I could not live without it now,' he said. 'This has got into my system.' He swept his hand out at the vast space of the world." [2]

But Wyoming also had another characteristic important to the making of the cowboy: it was distant from the civilizing institutions—law, in particular. The cowboy, especially in his early days, appeared to the rest of the country as a borderline character between law and outlawry. When cattlemen and sheepgrazers clashed, for example, the dispute was settled outside the law very often, a necessity explained this way by a character in a Eugene Manlove Rhodes story:

> "There ain't really no right to it. It's Uncle Sam's land we . . .
> graze on, and Unkie is some busy with conversation on natural
> resources, and keepin' republics up in South America and down in
> Asia, and selectin' texts for coins and infernal revenue stamps, and
> upbuildin' Pittsburgh, and keepin' up the price of wool, and fightin'
> all the time to keep the laws from bein' better'n the Constitution,
> like a Bawston puncher trimmin' a growin' colt's foot down to

1. Joe B. Frantz and Julian E. Choate, Jr., *The American Cowboy: The Myth and the Reality* (Norman: University of Oklahoma Press, 1955), p. 6.

2. Owen Wister, *The Virginian: A Horseman of the Plains* (New York: Macmillan Co., 1904), p. 75.

fit last year's shoes. Shucks! *He* ain't got no time to look after us. We just got to do our own regulatin' or git out." [3]

Wyoming earned its sobriquet, "the Cowboy State," during the days of the fenced range and the settled ranch. But the state also shared in the era of the great trail herds, which began in earnest after the Civil War. The longhorns were bred on the great open plains of Texas, then driven northward to fatten up on the rich grass of Wyoming and Montana before being shipped to market. The demand for beef grew out of the need to provide for Indians on the reservations, but those in military posts and the eastern population also became markets.

The cowboys who came on the drives were just that—drovers of cattle, not primarily fighters. The drives were organized with a foreman, several "hands," and a cook. Each rider had several horses—one for cutting animals out of the herd, another for night riding, still another for everyday purposes, and so on. The men (definitely males, no women, but some boys) took turns at duty during the night, except when catastrophes intervened. If the cattle stampeded, the entire crew was called out (or voluntarily jumped up to avoid being trampled to death) to turn the cattle and round them up, a process that often called for men to remain in the saddle for as long as a day and a night at a stretch.

The cattle themselves could hardly be called romantic. The Texas longhorn (*Bos texanus*) was descended from stringy brutes the Spanish brought over, with other strains mixed in after arrival in the Western Hemisphere. Their enormous horns often spread as wide as six feet or more from tip to tip. Some were solid in color—gray, blue, white, red, brown, black—others were mottled and spotted. Not noted for intelligence, the beasts could be alert and curious, and cows were fiercely devoted to the care of their offspring. They were not sociable toward humans but tolerated them. They responded best to direct force or commands—the cowboys on the trail carried

3. Eugene Manlove Rhodes, *The Rhodes Reader: Stories of Virgins, Villains, and Varmints*, ed. W. H. Hutchinson (Norman: University of Oklahoma Press, 1957), pp. 66–67.

their pistols mainly to shoot across the faces of the lead cattle in order to turn them during stampedes. The cowboy, whose job was to transport cattle, was challenged by a task requiring patience, endurance, and agility.

Some idea of the monotony and grim drudgery of this work, in contrast to the glamor associated with the stereotype, can be gained from an early narrative when cattle were driven through north Texas and Indian Territory to Kansas:

> (May) 8th. All 3 heards are up and ready to travel off together for the first time travelled 6 miles   rain pouring down in torrents and here we are on the banks of a creek with 10 or 12 ft water and raising   crossed at 4 Oclock and crossed into the Bosque Bottom   found it 20 ft deep   Ran my Horse into a ditch and got my Knee badly sprained—15 miles.
>
> 9th. Still dark and gloomy   River up   everything looks *Blue* to me   no crossing to day cattle behaved well.
>
> 13th. Big Thunder Storm last night   Stampede lost 100 Beeves hunted all day   found 50   all tired. Every thing discouraging.[4]

The days of the trail drive lasted until the railroads built better connections across the West and into Texas itself. By the 1880s Wyoming had plenty of cattle—though breeding and importation of Herefords and Shorthorns improved on the original stock—and cowboys became regular employees of the ranchers who ran cattle the year round.

The ranch owner occupied a spread of several thousand acres, typically, and his cowboys did the work of this enormous business. Again under the supervision of a foreman, they rounded up the cattle in late May and June in order to brand calves that had been born during the spring. (Branding, still done with a hot iron in Wyoming, also involved the less rosy tasks of emasculating young bulls, thus turning them into steers, dehorning, and tending to medical problems of the cattle.) As the open

4. From "Driving Cattle from Texas to Iowa, 1866: George C. Duffield's Diary," *Annals of Iowa,* Third Series, 14 (April 1924): 241–262. Portions reprinted in Robert V. Hine and Edwin R. Bingham, *Frontier Experience: Readings in the Trans-Mississippi West* (Belmont, Calif.: Wadsworth Publishing Co., 1963), p. 246.

range turned into the fenced ranch, cowboys repaired fences and windmills, and later, pickups and tractors.

But the cowboy was only the individual expression of an entire industry. Behind the cowboy stood businessmen and land speculators and railroad men and other civilized types. So it is necessary to understand something about the cattle industry (for that is what it is) rightly to appreciate the place of the cowboy in his world.

Successful exploitation of the rangeland in the 1870s appeared to hinge on the amount of capital that had to be put into labor, land, and improvements. The livestock industry appeared feasible only if open-range practices were possible—that is, if cattle could shift for themselves all winter long without shelter and supplementary feed and water. The bison had fared all right, although most of them had migrated to lower, warmer country every autumn. Many small herds of cattle had lived through winters in Wyoming, Utah, and Montana in the 1840s, 1850s, and 1860s, but rarely had they been required to shift for themselves from fall till spring. Lacking more promising avenues to wealth, a few of the Wyoming pioneers decided to experiment with the open-range cattle business.

Miners in Colorado, soldiers at Wyoming forts, residents of the railroad towns, and Indians on Dakota reservations needed beef. Stockers could be obtained for ten dollars per head in Texas. Millions of acres of federal government range could be used free. It would be many years before the government could survey the land and regulate its use. Every spring the cattle could be rounded up and given a minimum of supervision until fall when some of them could be marketed, either locally or in the Middle West after shipment by rail.

It was no secret that Wyoming winters could be harsh. This fact had been well publicized ever since the fur trade era, and particularly during the railroad construction period. The recollection of Seth Ward, Fort Laramie sutler, that there had been only three really hard winters in thirty-two years had been reported in the press to reassure the doubtful. As luck would have it, the territory's first three winters were mild. The *Cheyenne Leader,* which began publication in September 1867, first mentioned cattle February 7, 1868: "We guess the 'cattle upon a thousand hills' round about Cheyenne must have the remaining grass pretty well gnawed off by this time, from the numbers of them we see made to depend upon that mode of sustaining existence . . . we would advise a little ration of hay." Editor Nathan A. Baker felt better about the livestock business when summer came. He said, June 17, 1868, that "it is to stock raising and mining that these vast plains . . . must look to their future," and added on July 6 that "Cattle, horses and mules which were turned upon these prairies last fall . . . came out fat in February, March and April."

Nelson Story had driven 600 Texas longhorns past Fort Laramie and up the Bozeman Trail into Montana in 1866 just before the Sioux blocked entry to the Powder River country. John W. Iliff, who had run cattle in Colorado previously and supplied most of the beef for the U.P. construction crews, brought a herd of Texas cattle into Wyoming near Cheyenne in February 1868 and obtained a government contract to supply beef to several military posts. Others followed. There were 8,143 cattle on the assessment rolls in 1870 and 19,687 in 1871. Probably less than half were reported to the assessors. The *Cheyenne Leader* reported on September 12, 1871, that "Immense herds of cattle are constantly arriving from the east." These were presumably Texas cattle picked up at Ogallala, Nebraska, where Texans had delivered them.

The *Laramie Sentinel* published a notice calling for stockmen to meet in Laramie April 15, 1871. Gov. John A. Campbell and Maj. Frank Wolcott came over from Cheyenne for the meeting. Formal organization of the Wyoming Stock and Wool Growers Association followed at a second meeting on May 30, in which Governor Campbell was elected president, Dr. Hiram Latham, secretary, and Luther Fillmore, treasurer. The Union Pacific Railroad's active interest is indicated by the participation of Dr. Latham, its surgeon and immigration promoter, and Fillmore, its division superintendent in Laramie. To complete the roster of officers, five vice-presidents were named, one from each of the territory's five counties.

True to its name the association welcomed all stockmen,

whether they specialized in cattle, sheep, or horses. The announced goals included co-operative buying, reduced freight rates, improved breeding, mutual protection, and advertisement of the territory's advantages for stock raising. The organizers may have got some of their ideas from the Colorado Stock Growers Association which had started in Denver in 1867.

The Wyoming stockmen changed their name to Wyoming Stock Graziers Association when they met next in Cheyenne in October 1871 to draft laws for consideration by the legislature. The following month they met with the house of representatives in the hall of the house, with Governor Campbell (association president) presiding. Speakers at the joint session included one past delegate to the U.S. Congress and four future delegates, the governor and a future governor, a justice of the territorial supreme court, Dr. Hiram Latham, and a Presbyterian minister.

The minister told the assembly that he had sent his board of home missions in the East an account of the wonderful year-round, open-range stock business and had received in return a warning that he had been imposed upon and must be more circumspect. The legislature listened to suggestions from the stockmen and soon adopted a law which listed heavy penalties for theft of livestock.

The destructive winter that some people had been expecting came in 1871–1872, with blizzards early and often. In December 1871 the *Cheyenne Leader,* which had blown hot and cold on the subject of winter grazing, blew cold again, reporting that "The stock of the country has been subsisting on Latham's letters on winter grazing and Kingman's essays on sheep culture for a fortnight past." Supreme Court Justice John Kingman owned some sheep. The *Leader's* disparaging comment exasperated editor Hayford in Laramie, who suggested that editor Baker was more interested in displaying his wit than in benefiting the country. Hayford conceded that much snow had fallen in November, more, he said, than in any entire winter in the past twenty years. Union Pacific trains were stalled in several places along the hundred-mile stretch between Medicine Bow and Cheyenne in the last week of December and the first week of January.

No one could tell what was happening to the cattle until spring, when the owners learned that their losses had been heavy. Iliff lost more than half of his cattle and Homer & Sargent lost all but six of their 2,250 sheep. Among the casualties of that destructive winter was the Graziers Association. Dr. Latham, who had done most of the early promotional work, lost so much money that he dropped out of the livestock business and filed for bankruptcy.

The sharp setback to the territory's most promising industry strengthened sentiment in Congress favoring abolishment of the territory. Yet, optimists dismissed the bad winter as abnormal, and promotion began anew, with new leadership. Cheyenne (in Laramie County) replaced Laramie (in Albany County) as the focal point of the industry. Newcomers in 1873 squatted on some of the remaining choice ranch sites along the streams between Cheyenne and Fort Laramie. Cattlemen around Cheyenne formed the Laramie County Stock Growers Association on November 29, 1873, adopting substantially the same goals as those of the defunct Stock Graziers, although interest in sheep had declined.

The Laramie County Association in 1874 introduced cooperative roundups, in which several outfits combined to work all cattle in a district at one time. In the spring "calf" roundup they gave each calf the brand of the cow it followed. In the fall they sorted the marketable cattle, so each owner could ship his own. The Laramie County Stock Growers Association rapidly expanded until it became the Wyoming Stock Growers Association in 1879.

A promoter, J. H. Triggs, in 1875 compiled a list of eighteen outfits, each of which had more than a thousand cattle, and identified fifty-one smaller outfits. In 1877 Robert E. Strahorn, whom the Union Pacific employed as a publicist for a few years, made it appear, without naming names, that he was giving financial reports of actual operations. In one case, for instance, he said that an original investment of $10,000 had yielded a net profit of $36,000 in three years. Strahorn explained that the cost of maintaining cattle amounted to only $1.75 per head in herds of a thousand, and only $1.00 per head in herds of ten thousand. A steer, he said, could be raised and marketed as a three-year-old at a total cost of only $4.50. Since cattle could be sold for $30–$40 a head, Strahorn's data, and similar data reported by other promoters, made the business very attractive.

Gov. John M. Thayer, like Campbell, whom he replaced in 1875, had investments in cattle. In 1877 he proudly announced to the legislature that cattle shipments out of the territory by rail had increased almost sixfold since 1873. These cattle, he said, had literally raised themselves, having been out on the range all winter without hay or shelter, and had dispelled all doubts regarding winter grazing. Some bankers were not convinced. When Charles A. Guernsey described how cattle were handled on the open range, a Boston banker told him that he would just as soon lend money on a school of fish off Cape Cod.

Accurate herd counts were almost impossible. When outfits failed to find as many animals as expected in a roundup, they assumed that some had been overlooked and would turn up later. A common practice was to tally only the calves branded during the spring roundup and to multiply by five to get an estimated herd total. Adding the number purchased, subtracting the number marketed, and writing off 2 or 3 percent for losses would give an imaginary "book count." Often the owners underestimated the losses because of weather, predators, and disease. Investors who bought herds by book count, in their eagerness to get in on a sure thing, might acquire only half as many cattle as they thought they were getting. A Cheyenne saloonkeeper is said to have wrung wry smiles from glum cattlemen whenever it snowed by assuring them that the books would not freeze.

Each cow required from 20 acres of Wyoming's best rangeland to 130 acres of its poorest. An outfit with 10,000 head needed perhaps 300,000 acres in the best grazing country of eastern Wyoming. Under all the applicable land laws a rancher in the late 1870s and the 1880s could obtain title from the government to no more than 1,120 acres, which was barely enough for thirty or forty cows. For most of the land he needed, the rancher had no choice but to squat on government land—use it free—which he was entitled to do until the government surveyed the land and decided what to do with it. Prudent ranchers secured title to part or all of the 1,120 acres available, using it for the ranch headquarters and to control part of a stream. Each head of a family could take 160 acres free under the Homestead Act of 1862; another 160 acres free under the Timber Culture Act of 1873; another 160 acres at $1.25 per acre under the Preemption Act of 1841; and 640 acres at $1.25 per acre under the Desert Land Act of 1877.

The commissioner of the U.S. General Land Office, S. S. Burdett, had warned in 1875 that trouble lay ahead unless the government permitted stockmen to buy or lease the land they were using. Big outfits, he said, would seize control of vast areas and would clash with intruders who could argue that everyone had equal rights on the public domain. Territorial Governors John M. Thayer and John W. Hoyt repeated Burdett's warning.

Maj. John W. Powell, after his famous surveys, recommended in 1879 that cattlemen be given 2,560 acres of semiarid land free. He recognized that there was a great difference between the amount of land needed for a farm in the Midwest and a ranch in the West. In fact, 2,560 acres of semiarid grazing land was worth less than 160 acres of Iowa farm land. However, promoters in the 1870s had challenged the Great American Desert theory so often that congressmen who should have known better decided that 2,560 acres was too much to give away.

Hoping to avert the trouble anticipated by Commissioner Burdett, the U.S. Public Lands Commission held hearings in the West in 1879 and 1880, all the way from Montana to Texas and from Nebraska to California. Of twenty-four members of the Wyoming Stock Growers Association only three were willing to pay five cents an acre for title to the lands they were using. Not one of them favored twenty-five year leases at one-half cent per acre per year. They voted unanimously to maintain the status quo. They said that "thus far self-interest has proved a safeguard against the heavy stocking of the range," but said also that "the question of whether grass will not disappear from these ranges with constant feeding is yet unsettled, and that the stock business will not warrant the investment of so large a per cent of capital . . . in what may in a few years be barren and worthless property.[5] They argued also that confining cattle in severe storms was dangerous, since they needed to drift in search of feed and shelter.

A portent of things to come was the 1880 report of eastern visitor Clarence H. Mayo that the Powder River Country was "the finest stock country" he had ever seen, but that from Mexico to Canada too many people were "crazy over the business" and it would be "knocked to bits within three years" because of overgrazing and winter losses.[6]

As Mayo had reported, the cattle craze was not limited to Wyoming, but Wyoming was unique in that it depended more on cattle than any other territory or state did. Only the cattle business had appeal. In the early 1880s cattle poured in from Texas, Oregon, and the Middle West, filling Wyoming from stem to stern. Sheep came, too, in smaller numbers. Livestock dwarfed all other economic activities. William Hale undervalued slightly the importance of the Union Pacific Railroad, coal mining, and the federal government, but not by much, when he reported to the secretary of the interior in 1883 that "Stock raising is the chief industry, comparing with all others about as 90 per cent to 10. . . . Cattle by the thousand roam in every valley and drink from every stream in the territory." [7]

Investors made loans on cattle at 1, 2, or 3 percent interest per month, entered partnerships with experienced ranchers, or organized limited liability corporations. British investors (Scots and English), not satisfied with diminishing returns received from their investments at home, were attracted to the western cattle business by promotional literature and reports from naive advance men. The pendulum which had swung too far toward

5. *Preliminary Report of the Public Lands Commission,* House Executive Document 46, 46th Cong., 2nd Sess., 1879–1880, 544–547 (Serial 1923).

6. Clarence H. Mayo Collection, Henry E. Huntington Library. Used with permission.

7. House Executive Documents, 1883–1884, vol. 2, 575–587.

the Great American Desert notion in Wyoming's thoroughfare phase now swung too far the other way.

Finding that they could no longer count on holding their great free pastures intact, the big cattlemen and corporations in the early 1880s expanded their holdings of patented land by inducing some of their cowboys to file on free homesteads and deed the land to their employers when title had been acquired. This procedure was illegal, as was the cowboys' failure to fulfill residence requirements. Narrow strips of land along streams were especially desirable because they made possible monopoly control of much adjacent land, which others could not use without access to streams. Ironically, the Homestead Act, which had been designed to encourage homemaking, was now being used to prevent settlement. Thousands of men swore falsely that they had complied with the law. Mixed private and public lands were enclosed with barbed wire fences, so as to deny access to other public lands and to water.

Instead of filing on lands for the benefit of their employers, some cowboys filed on homesteads for themselves and entered the open-range cattle business in competition with their former bosses. Rather than gather unbranded cattle for their employers, as they had done in the past, they put their own brands on them. Whether or not they stole stock from association members, they were suspected of doing so. The association denied them membership. Association inspectors at major markets confiscated their shipments, sold them, and sent the proceeds to the association.

Meanwhile, to protect herds of its members, the WSGA in 1884 had obtained from the territorial legislature the Maverick Law, which gave the association full control over unbranded animals (mavericks) found in the official roundups which they organized in thirty-two districts throughout the territory. Nonmembers soon found cause to complain that some of their cattle were being swept up by the big outfits in their official roundups.

Overcrowding resulted from high cattle prices, huge profits in 1882 and 1883, and too-effective promotion. By 1885 the territory had 2 million cattle—four times the amount six years before. The WSGA asked Congress to give stockmen legal tenure to the public lands they occupied. Easterners called the big cattlemen landgrabbers. Obscured in the controversy was the fact that many of the new settlers were really not farmers in the usual sense, but small cattlemen who were planning to do what the big cattlemen had done—file on a small acreage and run cattle on the public domain. The federal government found it difficult to combat illegal practices effectively because the land laws as written invited perjury and because the government never had enough field men to classify the land.

Few of the participants in this scramble for the Wyoming range were Wyomingites. Most of the investors in the cattle industry in the West came from the East. Similarly with the cowboys themselves.

Many of the cattlemen lived in cities or towns, rarely seeing their employees. In 1880, 35 percent of the cattlemen who were Wyoming residents lived in cities or towns, the largest number of them in Cheyenne. They would visit their ranches in summer, traveling in buckboards or buggies or on horseback. Other owners lived in the East or abroad, and rarely set foot in Wyoming. Had more of the owners lived on their ranches they might have become better acquainted with their hands, won their loyalty, and improved the odds favoring success in their enterprises.

During the winter perhaps half of the cowboys were unemployed. Some of them "rode the grub line," enjoying the austere hospitality of one ranch after another for a few days or a week at a time. Many others loafed around saloons and livery stables. The industry might have been more sound if the hands had year-round work at something more than a subsistence wage.

The cattlemen transacted business and relaxed in their clubs in Cheyenne and Laramie. Cowboys were not welcome in these clubs, nor were they looked upon with favor by most of the townspeople. Bill Nye, editor of the *Laramie Boomerang,* who reflected public opinion more than he shaped it, described the cowboys as farm boys who liked to get drunk on Saturday nights and shoot out lights on Main Street. One cowboy in twenty, he said, was brave when armed. They injured themselves more than anyone else with their revolvers, he added.

Joseph M. Carey, Wyoming's delegate to Congress, 1885–1890, thought better of cowboys than Nye did, although he agreed that most of them had grown up on farms in the East and Middle West. Carey on the floor of the U.S. House of Representatives in 1886 described Wyoming cowboys as brave and generous young men. This was the period when cowboys needed a defender, because most people, East and West, considered them to be uncouth ruffians. They had not yet emerged as folk heroes.

Owen Wister was not the first to write about the cowboy. Nevertheless, he probably did more than any other writer (Buffalo Bill, the scout *qua* entertainer, also did his share) to popularize the cowboy as folk hero. His Virginian represents a reasonably accurate picture of the western cowboy. He came from east of the Mississippi after the Civil War. He was taciturn and not refined in manners or speech. He had few scruples against violence and after hanging his friend, Steve, for rustling, vows he would lynch again if it were needed. Wister's tale does include romance, but Wister spent a great deal of time in Wyoming and was familiar with cowboy ways. Without the constraints of late nineteenth-century publishing norms he could probably have represented cowboy life more to our present taste. In his journal he repeats a conversation he has heard and then remarks, "In all this I omit many pungent expletives." [8]

Other writers of the period also attempted to relay the visceral quality of cowboy life. Eugene Manlove Rhodes emphasized plot and action and saw one of his stories produced on the old radio show "Suspense." Alfred Henry Lewis attempted to reproduce inflections and accent in dialogue and to the modern reader probably appears only slightly ridiculous. For example:

"As the Lizard makes his bluff his hand goes to his artillery like a flash.
    "The Lizard's some quick, but Cherokee's too soon for him.
With the first move of the Lizard's hand, he searches out a bowie from som'ers back of his neck. I'm some employed placin' myse'f

8. Owen Wister, *Owen Wister Out West, His Journals and Letters*, ed. Fanny Kemble Wister (Chicago: University of Chicago Press, 1958), p. 106.

at the time, an' don't decern it none till Cherokee brings it over his shoulder like a stream of white light.

"It's shore great knife-work. Cherokee gives the Lizard aige and p'int, an' all in one motion. Before the Lizard more'n lifts his weepon, Cherokee half slashes his gun-hand off at the wrist; an' then, jest as the Lizard begins to wonder at it, he gets the nine-inch blade plumb through his neck. He's let out right thar." [9]

In the twentieth century more popular writers have carried the cowboy legend even further. Zane Grey has been accused of writing in a stilted manner; but he rightly calculated the public's taste in the matter and perceptively omitted intellectual and historical complexities. His novel, *Wyoming,* remains undistinguished even by standards of Greyophiles. Louis L'Amour has been called "America's most prolific writer—one who has sold more western books than any other writer." [10] L'Amour supposedly has sold 65 million copies of books about the West. But he himself denies some of the romance of the West: "The gunfighter is completely overemphasized in the West," he has said, adding that shooting took place mostly on the "wrong side of the tracks" and that western towns were not typified by gunplay.

But the movies have done more than any other medium to romanticize the cowboy. On the trail, the cowboys used to sing to the cattle because sudden noises startled herds and often caused stampedes; this nocturnal nursery detail became blown up into the flamboyant singing cowboy. The violence on the frontier was turned into personal confrontations freighted with transcendental weight—"High Noon" became a cultural cliché for moral encounters. Wister's own story was retold many times. The actor Gary Cooper played the role of the Virginian in a 1929 film (one of the first talkies) and then enacted a similar character in the 1950s movie, *High Noon.* Another example was *Shane,* a novel incidentally placed in Wyoming and made into a movie in the 1950s. Wister had written of the Virginian:

9. Alfred Henry Lewis, *Wolfville* (New York: Garrett Press, Inc., 1969), p. 16.
10. "A Man Called Louis L'Amour," on *60 Minutes,* CBS-TV, Nov. 14, 1976. Narrated by Morley Safer.

Then for the first time I noticed a man who sat on the high gate of
the corral, looking on. For he now climbed down with the
undulations of a tiger, smooth and easy, as if his muscles flowed
beneath his skin.[11]

Jack Schaefer later wrote in *Shane:*

Every line of his body was as taut as stretched whipcord, was alive
and somehow rich in immense eagerness.[12]

The quintessential man of the West, the strong, silent type,
the peaceful man who could become a raging fury when confronted with injustice—all this the movies took and presented as
cowboy, as true American male.

And the reality? The violence certainly existed, but show-
downs at high noon on Main Street were rarely as frequent
or dramatic as Hollywood led viewers to believe. In 1877 Jim
Levy and Charlie Harrison met in Shingle and Locke's Saloon
in Cheyenne, and because they had both been drinking, got into
an argument. Levy pulled a gun. Harrison, who had traveled
throughout the West and was known as an expert shooter, had
no weapon and asked Levy to wait until he could find one. Levy
obligingly waited, and later that evening they met in front of
Frenchy's Saloon. The two exchanged fire in the street. Some
six shots were fired, and Harrison was hit in the left breast. He
fell down and Levy, who had run across the street, fired, hitting
his opponent again, this time in the hip. Harrison died two
weeks later; Levy was arrested but apparently never tried. If this
description sounds more like a honky-tonk brawl on Saturday
night, it probably represents the actual situation. Harrison, like
many gunmen, did not shoot as well as he was supposed to, and
Levy played a most unheroic role.[13]

But that was only one incident, and Harrison and Levy were
not exactly cowboys. An apologist for the cowboys, William

11. Wister, *Virginian,* p. 2.

12. Jack Schaefer, *Shane* (Boston: Houghton Mifflin Co., 1949), p. 95.

13. Joseph G. Rosa, *The Gunfighter: Man or Myth?* (Norman: University of Oklahoma Press, 1969), p. 143–144.

Emerson Hough, claimed the cowboy could better be seen "as a steady, hard-working methodical man, able in his calling, faithful in his duties, and prompt in their fulfillment." [14]

According to many recorders, the cowboy richly deserved the stereotype that developed of the reserved, taciturn nonconversationalist. J. Frank Dobie wrote that cowboys frequently summarized events in succinct language that carried meaning despite its brevity. For example, he relates how two New Mexico cowboys followed noted badman Black Jack Ketchum and were attacked by Mexican border rangers, *rurales*. The Americans dispatched two of the Mexicans and reported their actions in the following manner: "Two of them *rurales* didn't need their horses any longer and we rode them out." [15] Wister acknowledges the same characteristic in the Virginian, who anticipates Gary Cooper's famed "yep" and "nope" in his talk. The cowboy's language thus expressed his love of isolation, a disdain for the continual palaver of urban life, making him admirable precisely because he communicated through silence.

The communication could become subtle, especially when it involved sensitive folkways. The Virginian's friend, Steve, straightforwardly called him a "son-of-a ———," to the astonishment of Wister-as-naive-narrator-eastern-newcomer. The profanity was part of the code of ironic language used among intimates. When Trampas, the villain, uses the same term, the Virginian levels his famous line at his adversary: "When you call me that, *smile.*" The cowboy delineated social boundaries as carefully as any New England puritan or southern Bourbon.

Those boundaries did not expand very widely when it came to consideration of nonwhites. The tribalism of the cowboy could make him mean-spirited, cruel, and racist. Wister wrote that ". . . life in this negligent irresponsible wilderness tends to turn people shiftless, cruel, and incompetent." [16] But nonwhite

14. Emerson Hough, *The Story of the Cowboy* (New York: D. Appleton, 1922), p. 181.

15. J. Frank Dobie, *Cow People* (Boston: Little, Brown and Co., 1964), p. 97.

16. Wister, *Owen Wister Out West,* p. 112.

cowboys were so rare in Wyoming that they were accepted as equals and judged by performance. In 1880 among 669 cowboys only two were black and nine were Indian.

The cowboy's attitude toward his horse could best be described as ambivalent. On the one hand, he often grew devoted to a particular animal. Andy Adams relates his grief at giving up his favorite horse at the end of the trail in Wyoming (the hands took the train back to Texas). On the other hand, riders were typically hard on their animals. Hough asserted that "The horsemanship of the plains has absolutely no reference to the feelings of the horse. It is the part of the latter to obey, and that at once." [17] Because they spent much of their time in the saddle, it was said that cowboys could reach any object or perform any task with a rope while sitting on a horse. "The cowboy does not walk, and he is proud of the fact," Hough wrote.[18]

Another aspect of the cowboy's life has been treated more realistically in contemporary art and movies. The diet of men working the range or the trail depended on basic staples: flour, beans, coffee, beef for noon and night meals, sometimes bacon at breakfast, and syrup and dried fruit as a primitive dessert. In a word, plain food for plain men. The mark of the popular cook was his ability to make light sourdough biscuits and strong coffee—there being no such thing, one cook averred, as coffee that was too strong but only people who were too weak. The well-known "son-of-a-gun" stew consisted of the inner organs of a calf mixed in with any available vegetables and cooked until the ingredients became an indefinable glop. Steak was common, but cowboys liked it well-done and fried, not broiled rare in today's fashion.

Wyoming in its isolation and with its distant plains nurtured the cowboy as lavishly as the fertile valleys of Fresno and Willamette nurtured the truck farmer and orchard grower. It was a natural symbiosis, one way that a state with few people could condition those few hardy men and women who chose to stay there. Yet cowboys were the hired hands, and the owners, ordi-

17. Hough, *Story of the Cowboy,* p. 64.
18. Hough, *Story of the Cowboy,* p. 53.

narily called "cattlemen" or "stockmen," followed a different, more typically bourgeois life, and saw the problems of Wyoming in a larger and more businesslike perspective.

Being a cattleman himself (residing in Cheyenne) and former president of the WSGA, Delegate Joseph M. Carey felt keenly the many aspersions cast by easterners on the integrity of western cattlemen. Cattlemen, he insisted, were just as honorable and upright as congressmen. When Carey described the age as one of "demagogism," an unidentified member of the House interjected "the age of brass." [19] Both Carey and the congressman who thought Carey represented the age of brass were right. Rugged individualism, aggressiveness, fierce competitiveness, and brass were prominent characteristics of the age in both eastern and western America.

There was, however, a growing national disposition to curb monopolies and trusts. Also, opposition to "cattle barons" stemmed from the fact that most of the people in the nation were farmers who had been brought up on the idea that farmers inevitably replaced cattlemen at one stage of frontier development.

A hot, dry summer in 1886 set the stage for disaster. The overstocking and overgrazing which stockmen had worried about for several years left almost no grass to carry the cattle through the winter. The fierce winds, which usually are relied on to clear the snow from parts of the range, were fiercer than usual that winter, yet they failed to move enough of the deep, crusted snow to make grass and water accessible. Many animals died from lack of water before starvation could overcome them.

The winter of 1886–1887 may have been no worse than the one of 1871–1872, but this time there was less grass, and forty times as many cattle. Three or four hundred thousand cattle must have died in Wyoming out of 2 million; and those that survived were in poor condition, many of them hardly worth shipping to market. The calf crop was very small. A thousand-pound steer that might have brought $60 in Chicago in 1882

19. U.S., Congress, House, *Congressional Record*, 49th Cong., 1st Sess., 1886, 17, pt. 6:6291, June 29, 1886; and Appendix, June 29–30, pt. 8:239–241.

sold for $10 or $15 in September 1887, not much more than the freight bill. Many outfits went broke. Membership in the WSGA dropped from 443 in 1886 to only 68 in 1890. The industry had been ripe for a fall. The steadily declining market since 1883, overexpansion, overgrazing, purchases on book count, high interest rates, absentee ownership, and poor management had led inexorably to disaster.

Small operators withstood the troubles of 1886–1887 more successfully than the big operators, perhaps because they were closer to their cattle, knew what was going on, and reacted quickly. Some of them not only survived but capitalized on the opportunities made available by the collapse of the large outfits.

By coincidence, the governor of Wyoming Territory in 1887 was Thomas Moonlight, a Kansas Democrat appointed by President Grover Cleveland, and a foe of the big cattlemen. Moonlight took pleasure in the distress of the cattle barons. He was the first Wyoming governor who avowedly wanted to break up the pattern of huge ranches. Echoing John Wesley Powell's recommendations, he wanted combination farming-ranching units consisting of 160 to 1,120 acres of deeded land on streams, with limited grazing rights on adjacent public lands. In his attempt to reorganize the cattle business, Governor Moonlight could do little more than the hard winter had already done, before a stockman, Francis E. Warren, replaced him in the governorship. Warren, a Republican, who was appointed by President Benjamin Harrison in 1889, had no sympathy for Moonlight's reform program.

The stockmen, large and small, who carried on, did not lose their political instincts. In the 1888 legislature six members of the WSGA sat in each house, and they were able to protect the association's major interests quite effectively. Thirteen stockmen were among the forty-nine members of the Wyoming constitutional convention in 1889. No other industry was so well represented. In the 1890 legislature, five of the twelve members of the upper house and nine of the twenty-four members of the lower house were stockmen. Theirs was still the largest and most important industry, although it no longer resembled a giant among pygmies.

The big cattlemen continued, and even increased, their complaints that thieves were ruining them. Unable to support as large a detective force as formerly, and not getting the arrests and convictions they thought they must have, a few cattlemen resorted to "do-it-yourself" tactics. By their actions they gave cattlemen in general a bad name. In July 1889 Ella Watson and James Averell were lynched on the Sweetwater a few miles east of Independence Rock. They had filed on homesteads in the middle of a cattleman's huge, government-owned pasture. Six cattlemen were arrested for the lynching, but witnesses disappeared, making convictions impossible.

The lynching of a woman was unprecedented. One of the six cattlemen said later that if "a woman put on the pants, she should be treated like a man." One woman lynched and one man's comments do not warrant a generalization about the attitude of cattlemen toward women. There is enough evidence, on the other hand, for the conclusion that in Wyoming, where women were scarce, most men, whether in the cattle business or not, were disposed to put virtuous women on a pedestal.

In November 1891 two men in Johnson County were shot to death from ambush. It was said that they had been stealing cattle. Although the local stock detective was suspected and accused of the crimes, he could not be convicted. Evidence suggests that a witness was silenced by intimidation.

In 1891–1892 a handful of big cattlemen had become so infuriated by cattle thieves in northern Wyoming's Johnson County that they secretly organized a search-and-destroy mission. The expedition included nine big cattlemen, thirteen ranch foremen, five stock detectives, twenty-two mercenaries from Texas, two newspaper reporters, and four observers. No Wyoming cowboy below the rank of foreman participated.

Fifty-two members of the party loaded a special train with horses and equipment and set out from Cheyenne early in April at the end of the annual WSGA convention. The train took them to Casper, where they mounted their horses and rode north. They were joined by three other men along the way. The "Invaders," as they were later called, hoped to surprise and assassinate twenty or more "rustlers." After they had killed only two

of the marked men, the Johnson County sheriff's posse sur-
rounded the Invaders until they surrendered to federal troops,
thus ending the "Johnson County War." Some of the captives
were charged with murder, but the case against them was dismissed in Cheyenne eight months later. Key witnesses who had
been spirited out of the territory could not be found by the prose-
cution. The Invaders had too many powerful friends in high
places, too much money, and too much legal talent.

Before the dust settled, the Invaders and the WSGA, whatever its role may have been, drew much criticism and some ridi-
cule all over the country. The importation of hired gunmen from
Texas drew special scorn because it was inconsistent with the
cattlemen's vaunted self-reliance. Some aspects of the affair,
such as the extent of the WSGA's involvement, are still obscure
and disputed because the 1892 records of the association include
no mention of it. Many Wyoming citizens who assumed that the
invasion was an official function of the association applauded
editor Hayford's comment that "of all the fool things the stock
association ever did this takes the cake." Association members
have maintained ever since that the invasion was an unofficial
project of some of its members.

Among the provocations that preceded the April 1892 invasion was the announcement in late March that the small cattlemen of Johnson County were going to hold their own independent roundups on May 1, 1892, just one month before the
scheduled official state roundups. Only the State Board of Live
Stock Commissioners had the authority to schedule roundups.
U.S. Sen. Francis E. Warren suggested later that the announcement by the small cattlemen of Johnson County could have been
used to justify a legal instead of an illegal invasion. Senator
Warren wrote to W. W. Gleason, one of his agents in
Cheyenne, on April 26, 1892, soon after the Invaders had been
disarmed and taken to Cheyenne:

> As you suggest, they ought to have the law behind them as they
> would have had in the attempted roundups, had they waited, and
> then the sheriff would have been obliged to be with them instead of
> against them. Militia Companies of state and Gov. could have
> followed, and in this case, if they should fight we could have used

the whole of the U.S. army, and yet the cattlemen would have been in the right and under the law, while the rustlers, etc. would have been against the law and criminally liable accordingly.[20]

Warren's letter refutes the popular excuse that the big cattlemen had exhausted all legal means of protecting their property. However, the Invaders were all ready to leave Cheyenne on April 5. For them to postpone their expedition more than three weeks would have been inconvenient, to say the least. What would they have done with their special train in the meantime? Had they waited until May 1 they might have been outnumbered and outgunned by the "rustlers" assembled for their roundups. Many of the Invaders could have been killed before the militia arrived.

After the Johnson County War the cattlemen were confronted by new challenges to their control of the range. Sheepmen had been overshadowed ever since the breakup of the short-lived Stock Graziers Association in 1872. Cattlemen had occupied most of the range in the late 1870s and early 1880s and had played the leading role in affairs of the territory. After the winter of 1886–1887 the wool industry expanded and moved into the vacuum created by cattle losses and bankruptcies. There had been some sheep losses but with closer supervision they had fared better than the cattle.

Most of the Wyoming rangeland is of intermediate character in that it has a mixture of forage crops that may be used equally well by sheep and cattle. Historically there have been shifts back and forth. Some stockmen will not change, while others will whenever it seems profitable to do so. Some cattlemen switched to sheep after 1887. Before long, sheep outnumbered cattle, although for many years they were not worth as much, because one cow was worth at least five times as much as one sheep.

Some of the woolgrowers lost money in the 1890s until the Dingley Tariff of 1897 provided protection against raw wool

20. Warren Letterbooks, April 26, 1892. In Western History Research Center, University of Wyoming. Used with permission.

imports and made the industry very attractive. It took less capital to enter the wool business. It did not take much money to put one or two thousand sheep and a herder on public land. The sheep cost $2 or $3 each. A herder could take his pay in sheep, and gradually build up his share of the band until he was ready to be a sheepman in his own right. In addition to resident woolgrowers with established bases, transient sheepmen moved through the territory, depending entirely on the public lands.

Cattlemen began appealing to the federal government for a leasing system and regulated grazing on the public domain. They probably assumed that they would be given priority rights on land they had been using. Sheepmen opposed leasing, except for some like Senator Warren, who had enough deeded land, state leases, and prospects for federal leases so that a leasing system would not hurt him. As usual, inability of the West to unite on a reform program meant that nothing was done. The discordant western voices, shouting "do this, do that, do nothing," reflected the diverse economic, environmental, and political interests of a vast, complex country. Also the high-handed behavior of a small number of cattlemen in the 1880s and 1890s caused congressmen, eastern editors, and many ordinary citizens in the West to smell monopoly in every leasing proposal. While they continued to call for leasing, some of the cattlemen employed violence to turn back the encroaching sheep. They hoped to be able to confine the sheep in desert areas where cattle could not utilize the shrub vegetation as well as sheep. They first issued warnings to sheepmen to stay out of a certain area. Then, as sheepmen moved into the forbidden zone, their flocks would be clubbed and scattered, while herders were tied up and sometimes killed.

In turn-of-the-century news columns one finds many reports like these:

May 1897. Jackson Hole cattlemen named a "committee of safety" and published notices that no sheep would be allowed to pass through Jackson Hole.
September 1897. One night, shots were fired into the tents of sheepmen who had crossed a deadline in the Big Horn Basin.

August 1899. Four disguised horsemen killed 150 of Senator Warren's sheep.

October 1899. The secretary of the state board of sheep commissioners said that the Wyoming range was "greatly crowded," yet hundreds of men were going into the sheep business and those already in it were buying more.

May 1901. Sheepmen in the Sweetwater country employed a band of mounted, well-armed men to resist attacks.

July 1901. A 13-year-old boy, Willie Nickell, was shot to death from ambush between Laramie and Wheatland. His father had introduced sheep into cattle country.

July 1902. One hundred and fifty armed men stopped fifteen herds of sheep that had crossed a deadline in the New Fork country of the Green River Valley, destroyed 2,000 sheep, scattered the rest, killed one herder, and drove out the others.

February 1903. A gang of masked men killed sheepman William Minnick and slaughtered 200 of his sheep between Thermopolis and Meeteetse.

March 1903. Seven masked men tied up a herder, burned his wagon, killed his horses, and slaughtered 500 sheep forty miles north of Lusk.

July 1903. National guardsmen from Basin restored order in Thermopolis where sheepmen had threatened to lynch a man held for the murder of Minnick.

November 1903. Tom Horn was hanged for the murder of Willie Nickell two years earlier. By common repute Horn was a hired killer.

April 1904. Sixteen masked men burned two sheep wagons and slaughtered 300 sheep south of Laramie.

June 1904. A sheepman was found shot to death south of Tensleep.

Such incidents occurred regularly for several more years.

Cattlemen claimed that sheep ruined the range, devoured everything to the roots, and crushed the roots with their sharp hoofs. They asserted that the very odor of sheep kept cattle from eating and drinking. Many unbiased observers have testified, however, that it is only the absence of feed that keeps cattle from going where sheep have recently cropped the grass. Estimates for the decade 1899–1909 indicate that cattle numbers rose from about 700,000 to 900,000 as sheep doubled from 3 million to 6 million. In 1908 and 1910 sheep were valued more than cattle. Generally speaking, cattlemen and sheepmen who had enough range from which they could exclude interlopers prospered during the first decade of the twentieth century. Two stockmen who did better than many of their contemporaries were Francis E. Warren, woolgrower, and John B. Kendrick, cattleman. Both had started with nothing and eventually became millionaires.

At the peak of the WSGA's power, during the "Cattlemen's Commonwealth" era of 1882–1886, woolgrowers had only a few feeble county associations to try to protect their interests. The county associations numbered ten in 1902. After absorbing many blows, which the county associations could not counter effectively, the sheepmen finally organized the Wyoming Wool Growers Association in 1905. By 1909 the association's 541 members had developed enough muscle to bring the aggressive cattlemen to book. The opportunity came after the "Tensleep Raid" of April 1909, in which fifteen masked men killed two woolgrowers and a herder near Tensleep in the Big Horn Basin. Backed by the National Wool Growers, of which Senator Warren had been president for several years, the state association was able to send five men to the penitentiary with sentences ranging from three years to life.

Fifteen men and a boy, and ten thousand sheep, had been killed in the range war. Other factors besides the Tensleep convictions contributed to the establishment of an informal entente. Both branches of the livestock industry suffered heavy losses from drought and overgrazing in 1910 and 1911, a destructive winter (1911–1912), and the impact of dry farmers in the years 1909–1914. Then, beginning in 1914, World War I brought exceptional prosperity to the cattlemen and moderate success for the woolgrowers. The number of cattle almost doubled, 1914–1918, while the number of sheep declined a bit.

As for the other adversary of the cowman, the sodbuster, there were some proponents of dry-farming in the 1890s and early 1900s. A bulletin of the University of Wyoming's College of Agriculture and Experiment Station assured readers, in 1909, that one-fourth of Wyoming "can be profitably farmed on natural precipitation by thorough practice of dry farming methods," and that, beyond that area, "practically all of the plow land" of one-half the state "will grow profitable crops by dry farming in a majority of seasons." The unwary reader might conclude that three-fourths of the state could be dry-farmed, overlooking the fact the author was discussing only "plow land," without mentioning how little there was. The author also neglected to mention the hot sun, wind, and inadequate rainfall of Wyoming.[21]

To the chagrin of the dry-farming promoters, critics responded to such exaggerations by quoting Bill Nye, pioneer journalist, who had written in Laramie in 1880:

> I do not wish to discourage those who might wish to come to this place for the purpose of engaging in agriculture, but frankly I will state that it has its drawbacks. . . . In the first place, the soil is quite coarse, and the agriculturist, before he can even begin with any prospect of success, must run his farm through a stamp-mill in order to make it sufficiently mellow. . . . Again the early frosts make close connections with the late spring blizzards, so that there is only time for a hurried lunch between. Aside from these little drawbacks and the fact that nothing grows without irrigation . . . the prospect for the agricultural future of Wyoming is indeed gratifying in the extreme.[22]

Providentially, not many farmers took advantage of the Dry Farming Homestead Act in 1910 and 1911, which doubled the amount of free land available under the old 1862 act, and those who did were discouraged by drought. Had the farmers been successful they would have attracted imitators. The disruption for the cattlemen and sheepmen would have been more severe, and the inevitable failure of the dry farmers would have been more massive.

For a short period in the 1920s, the number of settlers rose

21. November 1911 issue of the *Wyoming Farm Bulletin,* Laramie, Wyoming.
22. "Wyoming Farms, Etc., Etc.," *Forty Liars and Other Lies* (Chicago: Donohue, Henneberry & Co., 1890), pp. 202–204.

rapidly in Wyoming, but many of the homesteaders indirectly helped livestock men to enlarge their holdings, selling out to them at cheap prices or abandoning their homesteads without compensation. In the late 1920s, Wyoming Congressman Charles E. Winter dusted off an old claim for the "return" of all remaining public lands to eleven western states, ignoring the provision in the Wyoming constitution that Wyoming disclaimed all right to public lands as a tradeoff for statehood. Eastern congressmen were not ready to give up their constituents' interests and federal land, and Winter could not muster enough support from the western states because some of them would lose their source of funding for reclamation projects. So the proposal died. The Hoover administration at one point sounded out western people about ceding to the states the surface rights of public domain grazing land for the benefit of public schools. But stockmen were already using this land free, and Wyoming and other states wanted more than the surface rights. So this proposal, too, was dropped.

At this juncture, in 1934, drought, dust storms, and reports about how the stockmen were ruining the federal lands by overgrazing persuaded Congress to adopt the Taylor Grazing Act. This act, with a complementary executive order, provided that the federal government would terminate homesteading except on reclamation projects, retain permanently its remaining public lands, and regulate grazing thereon in the public interest as the U.S. Forest Service had been doing for many years on the national forests. Wyoming stockmen objected to passage of the Taylor Act. Eventually, however, stockmen found the Bureau of Land Management, which administered the new program, easier to deal with than the Forest Service.

The Wyoming stockmen never suffered more misery than they did in the Great Depression. Although use of the name Great American Desert had almost disappeared, the country had not changed. Some years were drier than others. A series of dry years came in the early thirties, with 1934 being the worst. Streams and water holes dried up. Dust covered everything. Grass and hay were almost nonexistent. In 1934 the federal government instituted an emergency cattle and sheep purchase program to minimize the disaster. In Wyoming, Agricultural Extension Service personnel were used to buy 25 percent of the cattle and 14 percent of the sheep at low prices. Most of the animals had to be destroyed, although some had enough flesh to warrant slaughter for the benefit of relief clients. Many stockmen were already on relief. The sales to the government gave them desperately needed cash with which to placate their creditors.

During these trying times the stockmen bitterly resented accusations that they were guilty of overgrazing government lands, and causing soil erosion by wind and water. No doubt there had been considerable overgrazing because the drought had severely depleted the grass and the stock had devoured everything in sight. With no market for the animals the only alternative to overgrazing that most ranchers could think of was to pray for rain. Secretary of the Interior Harold Ickes and Forest Service officials charged Wyoming stockmen with responsibility for erosion by wind and water, but the stockmen were blamed for more than they deserved. Dry farmers, whom the stockmen had tried to discourage, had contributed much more than the stockmen to erosion. Also, there had been much natural erosion.

Assailed by depression, drought, and government critics, the cattlemen closed ranks in the 1930s and co-operated more effectively than they had done since the nineteenth century. The WSGA increased its membership from 262 in 1930 to 2,102 in 1945. During the 1930s the proud cattlemen suffered at least as much as urban people. Even their vaunted self-reliance and independence eroded, as many of them broke down and accepted government assistance in various forms. The stockmen had to accept the government subsidy programs, some of them said later, "because everyone else was doing it." In Wyoming just about everyone was. The federal government spent $141,185,431 in the state, 1933–1939, which was more per capita than in all other states except Nevada and Montana.[23]

During World War II cattlemen prospered as they had not

23. Leonard Arrington, "The New Deal in the West: A Preliminary Statistical Inquiry," *Pacific Historical Review* 38 (August 1919): 315.

done since World War I. Yet many of them hated wartime restrictions, particularly price control on beef. They rallied around members whose grazing rights were threatened by plans to enlarge Grand Teton National Park. Still disgruntled after World War II, the Wyoming stockmen, in close co-operation with their national organizations, fired a barrage of complaints against Forest Service "bureaucrats" at various levels who lectured them on overgrazing and cut back sharply the numbers of animals they could graze on the national forests. Pleased with the extensive self-government permitted by the Bureau of Land Management, the stockmen wanted to amend the basic Forest Service Act to provide the advisory board system of the Taylor Act. In the next few years, however, one way or another, the Forest Service was able to win approval in the national if not the local arena, for its efforts to administer the national forests according to the principle of multiple use recognized in the basic National Forest Act of 1897.

Clifford P. Hansen, president of the WSGA, in convention in June 1953 gently admonished some of the more radical members of his organization:

> Recreation assumes more and more prominence. . . . The
> stockmen today finds that he is not alone in his interest in grazing
> lands. . . . Using public land in connection with private land, he
> knows that he is answerable for the care he gives this great
> resource. . . . He recognizes, always, that his interest must be
> dovetailed in with the public interest. Thus has been developed his
> civic consciousness.[24]

Hansen, who would be elected governor in 1962 and U.S. senator in 1966 and 1972, represented a new breed of more mellow stockmen. Also, he was speaking autobiographically—he held grazing rights in Grand Teton National Park. His statement to the stockgrowers in 1953 might have been greeted with mouth-filling oaths in previous decades.

After a long period, 1901–1940, of approximate equality with the woolgrowers, the cattlemen advanced to a position of un-

24. Maurice Frink, *Cow Country Cavalcade* (Denver: Old West Publishing Co., 1954), p. 224.

disputed leadership, faintly reminiscent of the 1880s. During World War II the number of sheep declined 21 percent and the number of cattle increased 27 percent. The shift to cattle continued after the war. In the 1950s roughly 60 percent of the cash agricultural income came from cattle, 20 percent from sheep, and 20 percent from crops—hay, wheat, sugar beets, oats, barley, corn, dry beans, and potatoes. In September 1976 there were about 1.6 million cattle and 1.1 million sheep, with the cattle worth close to ten times as much as the sheep. Wool prices were higher than usual but foreign competition, synthetic fibers, consumer dislike for mutton, the high price of lamb chops, and predator losses threatened to eliminate the sheep entirely.

As the twentieth century moved into its final quarter it became more obvious that the cattlemen had been right all along in thinking that most of the state should be left in grass. Gradually resentment against bigness diminished as people became aware of the efficiency of the larger units. The 1969 U.S. Census of agriculture reported that Wyoming had 268 ranches which averaged 40,000 acres in size, and 435 (including the 268) averaging 27,000 acres. There were also about 3,300 smaller ranches averaging 5,000 acres.

Most of the colorful stockmen of earlier years were gone. Absentee ownership increased rapidly after World War II as many ranches were taken over by corporations or, more often, wealthy individuals who were primarily interested in recreation, housing subdivisions, mining, water rights to be converted to industrial uses, or tax write-offs. Price tags on ranches had little relation to the value of livestock products. No one could buy a ranch and expect to realize from his livestock operation more than 2 percent on his investment, especially if the ranch had a good fishing stream and mountain scenery as a backdrop.

Most of the natives who know the cowboys best recognize them as hard-working men on horseback. The glamorous stereotype created by Owen Wister, which has been embraced enthusiastically by millions outside of Wyoming, has won considerable tongue-in-cheek support locally. The multiplication of automobiles and development of tourism gave rodeos a boost in the 1920s. Chambers of commerce began urging the natives to wear "western clothes" in summer. The Wyoming Department of Commerce and Industry took it up in the 1930s, asking everyone to wear "real western garb during the tourist season" and to "give our guests what they expect." Cajoled by many other promoters, most of the residents have complied, not because they are easily manipulated but because they find ten-gallon hats, colorful shirts, and cowboy boots comfortable and fun to wear, and because they know that tourism is of great economic importance.

The stockmen's record in a century of Wyoming politics is quite remarkable. Ever since they began seeking favorable legislation in the 1870s, many stockmen have made it their goal to try to control the state and local government. They have always had much, though rarely all-powerful, influence in the legislature. Quite often a majority of the members of the upper house have been members of the WSGA. At the close of the 1899 legislative session, a Laramie newspaper reported:

> A visit to the legislative chambers of the capitol reveals only a scene of silence and solitude. Where lately whirled the lariat, glowed the branding iron, or flashed the sheep shears, where cracked the whip of the cattleman and barked the dog of the sheepherder, all is now still and quiet. The hurly-burly of the roundup has passed and empty are the two big Wyoming legislative corrals.[25]

Before the late 1960s it was often said, with some exaggeration, that a bill had no chance in the legislature unless it was written on a cowhide or dealt with something that could be shipped, dipped, or clipped.

At least 80 percent of the stockmen have been Republicans. Since statehood in 1890 twelve of the twenty-one governors, half of the U.S. senators, and three of the fourteen U.S. representatives have been stockmen. Francis E. Warren and John B. Kendrick stood out as champions of their industry during their many years in the Senate. Wyoming was the envy of other western states in the 1920s when Warren was chairman of the Senate Appropriations Committee. During his thirty-seven years in the

25. *Laramie Daily Boomerang,* February 27, 1899.

Senate, Warren channeled much money to his state and over-looked no opportunity to place his friends on the federal payroll. He won appointment to the U.S. Supreme Court for his favorite Wyoming lawyer, Willis Van Devanter, who upheld his sponsor's economic philosophy constantly during his long tenure (1910–1937) on the court. Warren had a hand also in the spectacular promotion in 1906 of his son-in-law, John J. Pershing, from captain to brigadier general over 862 other officers. Although Warren was a Republican and Kendrick was a Democrat, they rarely differed on livestock legislation, and Kendrick's high-tariff voting record had few equals. Shrewd, successful nonstockmen in the Senate, notably Democrats Joseph C. O'Mahoney and Gale W. McGee, did not neglect livestock concerns and received considerable support from ranchers.

Cattlemen have been accepted locally as the custodians of the frontier spirit—personifications of self-reliance, independence, rugged individualism, and free enterprise. The same may be said for the woolgrowers except for one detail—they have been less self-reliant because they could not stay in business without tariff protection and import quotas. Whether they prefer cattle or sheep, the stockmen have stood for the work ethic, simple government, balanced budgets, and low taxes. Their economic philosophy generally has coincided with that of other interest groups. Dedication to self-reliance, however, has not deterred stockmen from seeking federal or state assistance in dealing with damage done to them by imports, drought, blizzards, wild game, grasshoppers, and predators.

For a long time the stockmen's success in winning legislative seats was in part a result of favorable apportionment. The U.S. Supreme Court eliminated that advantage in 1964 when it held that both houses of state legislatures must be apportioned on an equal population basis.

After 1964 political power gravitated toward the minerals producers and people dependent on them. While this was somewhat humiliating to some of the cattlemen who had so long enjoyed the center of the stage as the ruling elite, the power shift did not threaten the dominance of the traditional economic philosophy. The minerals producers were every bit as firm as the cattlemen had been in their opposition to big government, bureaucracy, big labor, and accelerating public spending. The cattlemen for many years had blocked imposition of a severance tax on minerals production. This was consistent with their traditional opposition to all new taxes. The fact that many cattlemen had enjoyed minerals income through leases and royalties may have influenced their votes. Whatever the motivation may have been, declining power did not change their attitude. On a key senate vote on a bill to increase minerals taxation in the 1976 legislative session, six of the seven members of the WSGA voted with the minerals-oriented legislators.

Wyoming continues to call itself the "Cowboy State" even though today's cowmen ride pickups more often than horses, and the cattlemen rely heavily on sophisticated management systems to assure a profit. But the cowboy image retains its meaning to many people in Wyoming because they are still able to take part in the happier aspects of range life—riding horses, raising livestock, and hunting. And denim, after all, remains a practical material.

Yet the culture's fascination with the cowboy carries some disturbing, not to say, pernicious aspects. The suggestion that a secretary of state can confront the enormous ambiguities of international policy by perceiving himself as a lonesome cowboy falters with only slight analysis. And the image of individualism associated with the "Marlboro" man and similar types hardly squares with the other-directedness so prevalent in the gray halls of corporate management. Looking in the rearview mirror may be enjoyable; but it can also be a distraction from the jarring realities of today's world. It also tends to distort the truth. Cowboys were not always admirable creatures; thrived only under the limited conditions of isolation and distance from society; and in the case of Wyoming cattlemen, easily surrendered their vaunted individualism when seeking the advantages of a special interest.

Wyoming liked the cowboy, and still does, mainly because he was one of the few who chose it as a place to live and work. Lonesomeness necessarily has that quality about it—not many people like it.

5

The Energy State

We want to strike a balance between the pressures for growth and development and the need to preserve our unique life style.

> —*Gov. Ed Herschler, December 1975*

One [hopeful sign] is a continued growth in the professional manager's sense of responsibility. The days are long past when he considers himself responsible to stockholders and no one else.

> —*L. G. Rawl, senior vice-president, Exxon, February 1976*

*H*ANDLING a really great influx of people was outside the Wyoming experience. In 1970 the population was only one-third of a million. The two largest cities, Cheyenne and Casper, each had about 40,000 people. Quite consistently the state had been the least industrialized in the nation, rarely exceeding 7,000 in manufacturing employment. For many years its exports had included its youth as well as its coal, oil, natural gas, and cattle on the hoof.

For a century—ever since the Union Pacific construction crews completed their work and retired from the scene—many residents, especially in the towns, had longed for economic growth, industrial diversification, more people. They wanted jobs for themselves and a bright future for their children. Some of the pioneers accepted any kind of development as long as it promised a payroll. Some stood ready to give tax breaks and other concessions to attract capital. Such subsidies sometimes ended in recrimination, as when a Laramie editor growled in 1892: "our citizens will not bankrupt themselves . . . and give everything they have made by years of struggle . . . and bankrupt our city and county with debt to put up for mythical schemes of impecunious adventurers." [1] It had taken a long series of disappointments to provoke this outburst.

The pioneers in 1870 guessed correctly that coal and livestock offered the best opportunities for growth. Coal was abundant, marketable, and not subject to the uncertainties of the open-range livestock business. The decision in the 1860s to locate the Union Pacific Railroad in southern Wyoming rather than along the central route through South Pass had been based mainly on the fact that extensive sub-bituminous coal seams had been discovered in the south. Under the Pacific Railway Act of 1864 the Union Pacific received mineral rights as part of its land grant. It fueled its locomotives with its own coal, and enjoyed considerable income from hauling coal to customers as far east as Omaha in the early years, and to many states, east and west, and even to San Francisco for export, in later years. Coal was the railroad's most important article of freight. The company's president testified in 1887 that coal had saved the road from bankruptcy. Important as coal was to the U.P. and to the territory and state, it left many pioneers disappointed and chagrined.

Only by a poor state's standards was coal a major industry. Six hundred men mined it in 1870. In the late 1880s close to one thousand men mined about 1 million tons each year for the U.P. at Carbon, Rock Springs, and Almy. Independent miners produced almost as much, most of it to be shipped on the U.P., although the Burlington had developed a bituminous mine at Cambria in Weston County.

Puny though it was by the standards of many states, the

1. *Laramie Sentinel,* March 5, 1892.

Wyoming coal industry was no abused, disadvantaged infant in its local context. In a poor, sparsely settled territory, two thousand jobs were of major importance and gave special status. The coal industry had political clout also because the U.P. owned the major mines and influenced the fortunes of independent mines that depended on the U.P. for transportation of their product to market. Although some legislators objected to U.P. policies and practices, they rarely blocked either the railway company or the coal industry.

Legislators enjoyed passes and other gratuities, such as excursions to Salt Lake City and Denver during legislative sessions. Proposals for taxing the coal output met stiff opposition. Several members of the constitutional convention in 1889 thought that a production tax of 1½ cents a ton should be placed in the constitution. M. C. Brown, president of the convention, reported that the territory spent $3,000 each year for a coal inspector and coal engineer, but received only $1,250 in taxes from the industry.

Spokesmen for coal argued that taxation should be left to the legislature, to which President Brown replied: "As you have seen in the past men elected to our legislature wearing the brass collars of the great railroad corporation, you will see just such men wear the brass collars of the great monied mining corporations." [2] Brown warned that coal was subject to depletion and therefore ought to be taxed before the deposits were exhausted.

Opponents argued that a production tax on coal would bring in more money than the state could use beneficially; the "infant" coal industry should not be discriminated against; the tax would be passed on to the miner and the consumer; such a tax would discourage capital investment; the coal counties (Uinta, Sweetwater, and Carbon were named) would vote against the constitution if it included the tonnage tax. Persuaded, the convention voted 17–9 to omit the tonnage tax. Although the constitution did include provision for a production tax on minerals "as may be prescribed by law," the legislature, as Brown predicted, failed to do anything about it for many years.

2. Henry J. Peterson, "The Constitutional Convention of Wyoming" (University of Wyoming Publications, vol. 7, no. 6, May 1, 1940), p. 121.

Just as the legislature refrained from taxing coal production, much of which was by the Union Pacific, so also it exercised restraint in taxing other kinds of railroad property. The U.P. kept much of its land grant off the tax rolls until 1887 by the simple device of postponing the patenting process. In 1907 a legislative committee found that Wyoming railroads paid taxes on 7 percent of the value of their property, compared to farmers and ranchers who paid 30 percent on farm lands and improvements, and 40 percent on livestock. Gradually railroad valuations were increased thereafter.

The U.P.'s coal lands were part of its 1864 land grant. The total land grant in Wyoming consisted of 4.5 million acres lying in the odd-numbered sections of a strip forty miles wide, twenty miles on each side of the railroad. Efficient mining required acquisition of some of the even-numbered sections which had been retained by the government. Denied the right to obtain the even-numbered sections legally, the U.P. borrowed a fraud from the cattlemen's repertoire, used dummy entries, and, like some of the cattlemen, had to accept dispossession and a slap on the wrist, pursuant to Justice Department proceedings instituted in October 1906.

The Union Pacific Coal Department's usual response to a walkout was to fire the strikers, import cheaper help, and call for federal troops to maintain order. When their pay was reduced from five cents to four cents a bushel in 1875, white miners at Carbon and Rock Springs struck and were promptly replaced by Chinese in the presence of troops requested by Gov. John M. Thayer. The U.P. gave the discharged miners free transportation to Omaha; it was an inexpensive way to avoid further trouble. The governor explained to the legislature that trains and mail must go through and the mines must be protected because they were necessary to the comfort of the people who lived along the line.

During the next ten years the company employed more Chinese than white miners. Resentment against the Chinese mounted because they worked for less pay and refused to organize. A riot (the "Rock Springs Massacre") resulted in September 1885, in which twenty-eight of the Chinese were killed, fifteen wounded, and several hundred driven out of Rock Springs. Most of the aggressors were British and Swedish immigrants who had been in the United States only a short time.

As soon as he learned of the riot, Gov. Francis E. Warren took a train to Rock Springs for a quick investigation. Then he wired President Grover Cleveland that an open insurrection prevailed, the territory had no militia, and troops were necessary to protect the mails and to arrest criminals. Just one week after the riot, federal troops escorted the fugitive Chinese back to Rock Springs, and some of the troops remained to protect them during the next thirteen years. The grand jury which was summoned presented no indictments.

A Sweetwater County representative in 1886 sought a legislative investigation of conditions in the Rock Springs mines. His request was denied although many people in the territory desired to terminate the employment of Chinese. Meanwhile there had been probes by the U.S. and Chinese governments. Eventually the U.P. found it impossible to continue its extensive employment of Chinese because the United States had suspended Chinese immigration in 1882, and Chinese replacements could not be found for miners who retired.

Had the U.P. been able to continue its reliance on Chinese miners, Wyoming statehood probably would have been delayed because the Chinese were not homemakers and state-builders in the usual sense. Their families lived in China, where many of the men wished to return as soon as they had saved some money. The hostility and the long, cold winters contributed to their desire to return to China. Like other coal camps in southern Wyoming, Rock Springs had no trees and almost no grass. Desert foliage—sagebrush, greasewood, and rabbitbrush—dominated the landscape. Water had to be hauled to Rock Springs from the Green River sixteen miles away. Wooded mountain ranges were so distant that the pioneer coal miners in Rock Springs could only dream of the delights which are sometimes said to be the birthright of all Wyomingites—trout fishing, picnicking in the woods, climbing mountains, and skiing.

According to coal camp folklore, the U.P. Coal Department (it became the U.P. Coal Company in 1890) valued a mule more than a man. In Wyoming, in coal mine disasters that occurred between 1886 and 1938, and that involved five or more men, 567 miners died, most of them in Union Pacific mines. At Hanna 171 men died in 1903, and 58 others died in the same mine in 1908. The U.P. and territorial and state governments did virtually nothing for widows and orphans. After the disasters of 1908 the U.P. Coal Company relented to the extent of paying a lump sum of $800 to each widow and $50 for each child under fifteen, enough perhaps to take care of them for a year or so. Children left with neither parent received only the $50.

Believing that such payments were inadequate, Gov. Joseph M. Carey in 1911 recommended that the legislature submit a constitutional amendment authorizing passage of a workmen's compensation act, like those other states were adopting in the progressive era. Carey was one of the state's few progressives, although he was a conservative Republican on most issues and was elected governor on the Democratic ticket. This versatile governor said that under the prevailing system only 29 percent of the damages collected in lawsuits reached the employees or their beneficiaries. Farmers and ranchers permitted submission of the amendment to the electorate only after they had been excluded from participation. Following approval of the amendment by the electors in 1914, Gov. John B. Kendrick (Democrat) recommended that just compensation be provided for, but cautioned the legislature "to avoid, so far as possible, the working of a hardship on the industry that pays the tax." In a subsequent paragraph, which dealt with the creation of a public utilities commission, Kendrick warned that "no greater injury could be done to the industrial life of our state at this time, than to enact a law that might be used in a spirit of hostility against the corporations." [3] Thus Governor Kendrick, a millionaire cattleman, reinforced the already friendly relations between cattlemen and corporate developers. The 1915 legislature increased payments to widows to $1,000 plus $60 per year for each child. The schedule of payments also included a lump sum of $1,000

3. Governors' Messages to the Legislature, Kendrick, 1915, pp. 7–8.

to a permanently disabled single man and $1,200 to a married man.[4]

The presence of petroleum was as well known as coal in pioneer days, but it remained essentially "neutral stuff," that is, raw material that could not be marketed in quantity at a profit, until the 1890s. Trappers had noticed "a great tar spring" in the 1820s. They told Capt. B. L. E. Bonneville, who in turn told Washington Irving, who mentioned it in his famous book, *The Adventures of Captain Bonneville U.S.A.* (1837). Oil seeps were reported often thereafter, particularly along the great central Wyoming trail. A flowing well was completed at a depth of 350 feet in the Dallas Field southeast of Lander in 1883.

A 1,000-foot well produced a quantity of oil in 1889 in the Shannon field in Natrona County 45 miles north of Casper. A cluster of wells in this small field led to the construction of a primitive refinery in Casper in 1894. Barrels of crude were hauled to the six-year-old village with string teams of horses. The refinery produced up to 100 barrels of lubricating oil a day, which was enough to saturate the regional market, there being few customers except the railroads.

Claims had been filed in the Salt Creek anticline just south of the Shannon field, beginning in 1883. Although a discovery was reported in 1889, production was delayed until 1908 when a gusher from the First Wall Creek Sand at 1,050 feet attracted new capital from California, Colorado, and eastern states. In the next seventy years Salt Creek, Wyoming's nonpareil field, would produce more than a half-billion barrels of high-gravity, green crude at relatively shallow levels.

After the first gusher, much litigation resulted from conflicting, overlapping claims, many of them of the dummy variety, filed under the mining laws of 1872 and 1897. Unless one camped on his claim with a force of armed men, another armed force would probably move or destroy the stakes and take possession. It was no place for a man without oil experience, capital, and gall. The rush to file additional claims and prove discoveries was interrupted by President Taft's executive order of

4. *Session Laws of 1915,* pp. 172–186.

September 27, 1909, which withdrew the Salt Creek area from location under the mining laws. Nonetheless, there was profit in the business during World War I for those who controlled the small amount of patented land and a leased school section, and soon after the war, the U.S. Oil and Gas Leasing Act of 1920 opened Salt Creek to leasing on a royalty basis. The small number of tough, ruthless men who had been able to hold their claims through the previous decade received priority leasing rights.

Now Wyoming once again held a treasure sought by the rest of the nation and the world. This time the stakes were much higher than those involved in the fur, cattle, or coal trade. Wyoming, far from the centers of population, had a chance to provide much of the fuel for the fabulous American car. And once again outsiders came to Wyoming, at first foreign investors, who fared poorly; but then Coloradans, who did much better with the Midwest Oil Company. They built a refinery in Casper and laid a forty-mile pipeline from Salt Creek. But the true descendents of the Astorians and cattle kings and railroad magnates showed up with Standard of Indiana, which entered Salt Creek in 1913 and captured control of Midwest in 1920.

Standard of Indiana for a few years solved the marketing problem by shipping gasoline from Casper to Baton Rouge by rail. However, completion of more wells overloaded the system and voluntary proration had to be adopted at Salt Creek thereafter.

Sharing leadership with Standard of Indiana in Wyoming was the Ohio Oil Company (Marathon), which began production in the Grass Creek field in the Big Horn Basin in 1914 and eventually spread all over the state. The Federal Trade Commission reported in 1921 that Standard of Indiana (AMOCO) and the Ohio Oil Company (Marathon) together controlled between 93 percent and 97 percent of production in Wyoming. "There is greater concentration in the control of production of crude oil in the Wyoming oil fields than in any other field in the United States," said the FTC report.[5]

---

5. *New York Times,* January 3, 1921, p. 12, col. 1.

The oil industry is capital intensive and not labor intensive. Drilling wells, operating refineries, and maintaining pumps takes relatively little manpower. Therefore, development of petroleum in Wyoming did not bring on hordes of jobseekers. However, oil fields created a scene onto which walked a new individualist reminiscent of the old trappers and the cowboys. The roustabout reeks as much of toughness as grease. His lore belongs to the machine shop and the toolbin rather than the forest and the plain. He has the hell-raising qualities of the old-timers but skills that belong to the industrial age. He is as mobile as the trapper, relying on pickup or car and house trailer to move where the jobs are. To work in the oil field requires standing out in all kinds of weather, day and night, to do a job. The difference with the trapper and cowboy is that in the oil field man is at war with nature, rarely comfortable with it. A trapper might have real ambivalence toward the grizzly, and the cowboy a downright dislike of the cow. But both of them in various ways had to make their peace with nature, to accommodate themselves to the weather, to receive what nature had to offer and take it on its own terms. The oil worker guides the diamond bit into the earth to suck it of its worth, and then leaves it. It is work involving little feeling for the land, little warmth toward something as inanimate as petroleum. But again, Wyoming is viewed, not as a place to live, not as a place to build cities, but as an empty space that contains within it something of value, something that capitalists and engineers and bureaucrats can manipulate for their own purposes.

A young sociologist, Robert S. Lynd, who would later become famous, spent three months as a roughneck in the Elk Basin field in 1922, earning $4 a day, less $1.35 for board. He wrote in *Survey* magazine that there was no water, trees, or grass where the employees of Standard of Indiana and the Ohio Oil Company lived in tents and tarpaper shacks. The men had a pool hall, but the women and children had no community hall. All pumpers, drillers, and tool dressers worked seven 12-hour days, with no overtime pay. Others worked seven 8-hour days or six and one-half 9-hour days. In camp there was little to do "but sit and look at the naked buttes." Those (about one-third) who had automobiles meandered twenty miles through the sage-brush to a movie or forty miles to a trout stream for brief respites. Employees earned one week of vacation with pay after a year's service. Fear of pay cuts or layoffs worried the men, none of whom belonged to a union. Lynd reported that "the men were most universally in favor of organizing but in mortal terror of the companies' finding them out." [6]

Given an opportunity to comment on the Lynd article, John D. Rockefeller, Jr., wrote that the 12-hour day and the 7-day week should no longer be tolerated, and better living conditions ought to be provided, but he was only a minority stockholder and in no position to change conditions. He added that the problems were deep-rooted because oil fields were temporary and speculative and therefore suffered difficulties greater than those of coal mines. [7] It appears that generally oil field workers were better off than coal miners; at least their lives were not snuffed out in wholesale lots by mine explosions—though the dangers of falling from derricks and of being hit by a rapidly revolving chain made the hard hat functional gear.

Many wildcatters found oil which they could not sell profitably. They grumbled about the low prices they had to accept from Standard of Indiana, which owned the refineries in Casper, Laramie, and Greybull. Pipelines were not yet available for marketing the independents' crude oil out of state.

A minor oil field, Teapot Dome, which is located between Casper and the great Salt Creek field, became world-famous in the 1920s. It was reserved for future navy use until the secretary of the navy, Edwin Denby, transferred it to the Interior Department, and the secretary of that department, Albert B. Fall, secretly and without competitive bidding leased it to Harry Sinclair. Alerted by a few independent oil men who had heard rumors of the lease, U.S. Sen. John B. Kendrick raised questions in the Senate which led to an investigation, and to trials in federal courts. U.S. District Judge T. Blake Kennedy, who had practiced law in Cheyenne many years before his elevation to

---

6. Robert S. Lynd, "Done in Oil," *Survey* 49 (November 1, 1922): 146.
7. Lynd, "Done in Oil," *Survey,* p. 147.

the bench, upheld the Teapot Dome lease to Harry Sinclair's Mammoth Oil Company. Judge Kennedy recognized that the terms of the lease were more favorable to Wyoming and the federal government than to Sinclair, who overestimated the richness of the field. Also, the lease called for a pipeline, which would have expedited the marketing of Wyoming crude oil. Judge Kennedy seems to have been less concerned about the fraud and bribery aspects of the case than was the Supreme Court, which overruled him unanimously. Eventually Albert B. Fall received a prison sentence for arranging the transfers of the Teapot Dome field and accepting a bribe from Sinclair.

The story of oil industry taxation in Wyoming is one of many postponements and much frustration for daring individuals who pushed for increases. Oil taxation followed the pattern set for coal taxation, and neither added much to state or local revenues for many years. Legislators accepted the arguments of lobbyists: the industry was an infant, wells would be capped, oil men would leave the state, there would be widespread unemployment, Wyoming was a high-cost area, great risks deserved high returns, and the taxes would be passed on to the Wyoming consumer.

The state board of equalization, which was created in 1919, after it had been authorized by a constitutional amendment in 1910, did increase the assessed valuation of oil considerably, placing it ahead of coal for the first time in 1920 ($19 million for oil and $15 million for coal). Regularly thereafter the total valuation of oil exceeded that of coal. In 1924 oil produced by the Midwest Company (Standard Oil) was assessed at $1.15 per barrel. Gas was valued at three cents to seven cents per thousand cubic feet.

In 1923 Gov. William B. Ross (Democrat), a Cheyenne lawyer, whose 1922 platform had included a plank which called for making corporations "bear their fair share of taxation," asked for a severance tax on oil. The request came at a most propitious time. No one could deny that oil appeared to be doing better than all other segments of the Wyoming economy. All major industries other than oil—agriculture, livestock, railroads, and coal—were obviously suffering from postwar deflation, while oil production records had been set every year for several years in a row. Oil made up 61 percent of the state's products valuation in 1923. Drought compounded rural distress, and many banks that could not collect on farm-ranch loans were about to go broke.

As usual, conservative Republicans controlled both houses of the 1923 legislature with substantial majorities. Although new taxes were normally anathema to them, their concern about the ability of depressed industries to pay existing taxes caused them to drop their guard when the new, absentee-owned source of revenue was mentioned. Contributing to the drive for a severance tax was the common belief that the United States and Wyoming oil reserves were quite limited. The director of the U.S. Bureau of Mines in 1920 had predicted that at the current rate of consumption available reserves would be exhausted in eighteen to twenty years. The state geologist of Wyoming expressed the same opinion in 1922. Legislators argued that a special tax should be collected and a fund created to cushion the impact that must come when the oil industry and its transient operators left the state. Such a tax had been collected in Louisiana for several years.

Members of both parties introduced severance tax bills. A 1 percent proposal introduced by an Albany County cattleman, Republican John A. Stevenson, was favored before it was defeated by the argument that it was probably unconstitutional. The legislature then agreed to submit a constitutional amendment providing that "there shall be levied a severance license tax based on the actual value of the gross product." Although the electors in 1924 favored the amendment by a majority, it failed to pass because the Wyoming Supreme Court had decided in 1910 that a majority of the electors meant not a majority of persons who voted on the amendment but a majority of all persons who voted in the election—a decision requiring the amendment receive more votes than it did. By their decision in 1910, which had nothing to do with oil, the Wyoming judges made it possible to postpone the collection of a severance tax until 1969—forty-five years.

The death of Governor Ross in October 1924 and falling oil

production for ten years beginning in 1924 dampened enthusiasm for a severance tax. Had the amendment, which won such a large majority from those who voted on it, been adopted in 1924, it probably would have been blamed for the decline in production which had already set in. Flush production in Texas, Oklahoma, Kansas, and Louisiana, however, was mainly responsible for Wyoming's sharp drop from 44 million barrels in 1923 to 11.5 million in 1933.

However, the market for gas in the 1920s was even worse than it was for oil. Yet the gas came up with the oil, and technology had no economic way to separate the two. The result was a practice known as "flaring," whereby gas was burned at the wellhead. To have released it into the air without burning would have created a danger of explosions. The outsider who passed through a field where flaring was done witnessed a strange scene, especially at night. Flames leaped high into the air and the fumes laced the ozone with their carbon, creating an inferno-like wasteland more appropriate to the industrial East than the desert West.

Flaring was practiced not only in Wyoming, but in Texas and other parts of the country, well up into the 1950s. The alternative would have been to cap the wells and hold both the oil and the gas for the future when markets could have been found for both. But to have taken this route would have kept the oil companies from marketing the oil and would also have meant unemployment because the refinery in Casper would have been shut down. Flaring was accepted, then, as the price for doing business.

As markets were found, and pipelines installed to Denver, Billings, Salt Lake City, and various points in the Middle West, Wyoming's oil output increased 300 percent between 1933 and 1947 and its gas, 60 percent. Oil and gas production rose even more sharply thereafter, while coal output dwindled as it was replaced by clean, convenient, and cheap natural gas almost everywhere except in railroad locomotives, which substituted diesel fuel for coal in the 1950s.

Wyoming residents expected the oil companies to pass taxes on to consumers, yet did not think much of the added burden would be collected from Wyoming consumers when more than nine-tenths of Wyoming oil was consumed outside the state. They have always resented the fact that gasoline prices are two to ten cents higher in Wyoming than in surrounding states where little oil is produced. Attempts were made in the 1930s to reduce prices, and gasoline prices receded two or three cents a gallon before World War II sidetracked the issue.

Until the U.S. Supreme Court outlawed it in 1948, the "Tulsa plus" pricing system was often blamed for Wyoming's high gasoline prices. The "Tulsa plus" system meant that oil companies set a base price to be charged in Tulsa and then added the freight between Tulsa and other cities in the region to determine the retail price for each city. The Supreme Court may have ended the "Tulsa plus" system but did not stop retailers from charging more for gasoline in Wyoming than in neighboring states.

The state minerals supervisor reported in 1951 that Wyoming was far behind "more enlightened and progressive" states in conservation. Although most major oil companies conceded that something ought to be done, they used the needs of independents to excuse inaction. It was asserted that many small independents could not bear the increased costs of mandatory conservation. To placate them it was specified in a compromise act adopted in 1951 that the industry would not have to bear the cost of enforcement. Also limitations on flaring were made meaningless by a provision excepting "gas unavoidably produced if it is not economically feasible for the producer to save or use such gas." Four years later Wyoming finally joined the Interstate Compact for Conservation of Oil and Gas. To do so, however, the legislature first had to tie the hands of the executive and judicial branches by including a provision that "this Act shall never be construed to permit or authorize the Governor, or any court to make, enter or enforce any order, rule, regulation or judgment requiring restriction of production of any pool or of any well to an amount less than the well or pool can produce." [8]

8. *Session Laws of Wyoming of 1955*, p. 117.

The reluctance of legislatures and governors to tax the coal and oil industries and to impose conservation measures was not due entirely to the persistence of eighteenth-century economic theory, powerful lobbies, and gullible legislators. There was some truth in assertions that developers were handicapped by an unfavorable climate, great distances from markets, jumbled geological strata, and high costs. Moreover, the recurring plea that there is no need for more revenue was not invented by energy resource lobbyists. Most of the people in Wyoming until World War II had known more bad years than good. With them it was an article of faith that there should be no additional tax before a compelling need arose. Not many social services have been considered to be compelling needs in a society which boasts of self-reliance. Commonly the unemployed and welfare recipients were faulted for their plight. Just as Wyoming was the last state to ask for federal assistance to take care of its needy in 1933, so also the ratio of welfare recipients to the rest of the population has been consistently low in comparison to other states, and payments per recipient have been well below national averages.

After World War II some Democrats who wanted additional state services thought the oil industry looked prosperous enough to bear a severance tax. Although other major oil-producing states generally had severance taxes, the Wyoming oil men were so well-entrenched politically that they could turn back all proposals. Normally they could count on support from legislators representing the minerals-rich counties. The cattlemen who previously had been divided on the issue swung over to the industry side. Unlike the situation in some other oil states, the powerful cattlemen had offered little opposition to development, partly because the state's major fields lay in barren areas where there were few cattle; so it was not difficult for them to defend the oil industry at mid-century. Prominent cowman J. Elmer Brock warned that levies on oil would be followed by similar taxes on cattle and sheep. Depletion worries had disappeared; so the urgency to tax before it was too late was gone. There seemed to be vast reserves, much unexplored territory, and the technology with which to plumb depths previously beyond reach. Overoptimistic reports from the U.S. Bureau of Mines oil shale research laboratory in Laramie fostered the belief that when the oil wells ran dry, oil shale could satisfy the needs for many years.

Many influential men, some of them in the legislature, had income from oil. Roadblocks went up whenever a severance tax bill was introduced. One obstacle was the constitutional provision that "All taxation shall be equal and uniform." It was argued that all minerals must be treated alike, and that production of some minerals other than oil would be unprofitable if taxed. Special solicitude was also expressed for marginal independent oil producers.

Whenever the question came up in the legislature, it was argued that the severance tax problem was complex and should not be touched without a special study. The legislators, who (before 1974) were in session for only forty days in odd-numbered years, had no time for the study, and chose not to authorize a study by experts. Unauthorized studies were swept under the rug. University of Wyoming professors were told by President G. D. Humphrey to keep hands off because it was outside the university's proper sphere to tell the legislature who should be taxed. When teaching at the university in 1945, Velma Linford mentioned the term "severance tax" in a radio talk. Her locked office door was opened and searched that night, presumably for the text of her remarks, but she had spoken without notes.

Gov. Joseph M. Carey in 1911 had recommended the creation of a nonpolitical tax commission to study taxation and revenue and to advise on such matters, but the legislature had ignored him. Later the state board of equalization, which was created in 1919, filled part of the gap. But not until 1971 was the legislative service office established to give expert assistance in such matters.

Although the Wyoming oil industry defeated all severance tax proposals for many years, it paid property taxes which may be regarded as severance taxation without the name. Beginning in 1919 oil production has been assessed at 100 percent of the posted field price in lieu of assessment on the land (mineral deposit). In 1940 the evaluation of the oil product amounted to about 5 per cent of the state's total property valuation. This increased in the 1960s until more than 39 percent of the property tax revenue was collected from oil and gas. In the leading oil counties the industry paid most of the property taxes. Also, 37½ percent (50 percent after August 4, 1976) of the royalties collected by the federal government from production on its property was returned to the state of origin under the Oil and Gas Leasing Act of 1920. This amount would exceed $40 million in 1976. Furthermore, some of the royalty money retained by the federal government had been used by the Bureau of Reclamation to build projects in Wyoming. Even so, the state minerals supervisor was probably correct when he said in 1954 that the Wyoming tax structure was as equitable or more equitable (for the producer) than that of any other major oil-producing state.

The hold-the-line policy finally broke down in 1969. Since 1935 the state's major source of general fund revenue had been a sales tax, set at 3 percent in 1967. When still more revenue was needed in 1969, oil industry leaders reluctantly accepted a 1 percent severance tax without making a last-ditch fight. It looked like the lesser of two evils after an income tax had been suggested as an alternative.

In 1969 sodium sesquicarbonate (usually called trona in Wyoming), uranium, iron ore, and coal mining all looked prosperous enough to pay a 1 percent tax in addition to the property taxes they were paying. The oil industry could no longer hide behind these thriving infants. Problems in almost all other segments of the economy made it impossible for the relatively rich oil industry to dodge a severance tax any longer.

Agents of state government and representatives of chambers of commerce zealously pursued industrialists who might build new manufacturing plants, but to little avail, in the 1960s. The reasons had less to do with taxes and economics than weather and isolation—Wyoming's old bugaboos. In 1963 twenty-five Chicago-based firms in reply to queries from the state's Natural Resource Board explained that they had never considered locating branch plants in Wyoming because its weather was too severe. Neil Morgan in his book *Westward Tilt* observed in

1963, "Except for Alaska there is no American state on which the passage of time and man has left so small an imprint as Wyoming." Later in the decade the *Wall Street Journal* described the state as "The Lonesome Land."

Just how lonesome was shown by the 1970 census: the state had only 332,416 people, ranked 49th among the states, had gained only 2,350 people between 1960 and 1970, and was being overtaken rapidly by the 50th state, Alaska. Manufacturing payrolls added up to no more than 7,000. The capital-intensive raw materials producers employed relatively few workers. The railroads carried more freight with a much smaller work force than formerly. Expansion in tourism, personal services, trona mining, and government did little more than offset losses elsewhere.

Prospects for development looked no better in the early 1970s than before. Only a few super-optimists expected the oil and gas industry to expand further. No great field had been discovered since 1918. Nine thousand wells were producing in twenty-two of the state's twenty-three counties. Most of the wells had produced enough to pay their original costs many times over but could not be expected to continue indefinitely. Cumulative production approached 4 billion barrels as the proved reserves dropped below 900 million barrels. After a record output of 156 million barrels in 1970 the anticipated decline began, several million barrels each year. Natural gas production peaked at 384 trillion cubic feet in 1971, and also began to decline. At the 1971 rate of production the proved oil reserves amounted only to a six-year supply, and the gas reserves to a ten-year supply. However, some 100 rigs continued to probe for new oil and gas, sometimes to depths in excess of 20,000 feet, and at a cost of more than $5 million per well. Minor discoveries were made every year; so the inevitable exhaustion might not come, it was thought, before the year 2000.

But international events interceded unexpectedly somewhat as they had done in the days of the fur trade.

In the 1960s only further stagnation could be foreseen for the next decade, except in Campbell County, where most of the new oil was concentrated, and Sweetwater County, where trona mining and refining flourished. Then suddenly the October 1973 Arab oil embargo and the subsequent quadrupling of oil prices by the Organization of Petroleum Exporting Countries (OPEC) swept stagnation aside. The average price of Wyoming crude oil tripled. The price of uranium leaped from $8 to $40 per pound. Much "neutral stuff"—deep pockets of natural gas in southwestern Wyoming, low-grade uranium ore, and great beds of low-grade coal—turned into valuable natural resources. Wyoming ranked fifth among the states in oil production, seventh in natural gas; first or second in uranium production and reserves; first or second in coal reserves; and third in oil shale. Especially because of its coal reserves Wyoming was recognized as one of the greatest, if not the greatest, of the nation's energy states. To many observers it appeared that the poor, have-not state had struck it rich. To others Wyoming appeared to be threatened with destruction.

In the winter of 1973–1974 the nonresidents who owned most of Wyoming's bonanzas were recalculating their net worth; and the residents who were not skiiing, riding snowmobiles, or fishing through the ice for recreation were forecasting the fallout and spillover effects of the energy crisis. Most residents expected an influx of people such as had never been seen in the state before. Among the predictions were the release of much imprisoned natural gas by fracturing tightly packed sandstone with underground nuclear explosions; the erection of one or more uranium enrichment plants; the production of vast quantities of oil from shale; stripmining of billions of tons of coal; construction of fifteen huge coal-fired steam power plants and fifteen coal gasification or liquefaction plants; the overcrowding of many communities; intolerable pollution; destruction of scenery, fishing, wildlife, and the tourist industry; the end of farming and ranching; the loss of Wyoming's traditional lifestyle; and the ultimate conversion of the state into a new Appalachia, a wasteland, or a "ghost state."

A few of these predictions soon proved to be wrong. Residents of the state's least populous county, Sublette, won their battle to persuade the Atomic Energy Commission and El Paso Natural Gas not to use nuclear explosions near Pinedale in an effort to stimulate natural gas flow. The prediction that Reynolds Metals Corporation would build a uranium enrichment plant in Johnson County ended in 1973 when the corporation sold to Texaco most of the land, coal, and water rights it had acquired over a period of a decade. It was surmised that Texaco was more interested in coal gasification than uranium enrichment. Three years later Texaco's bid for participation in an experimental government gasification plan was rejected in favor of sites in Illinois and Ohio, and Johnson County people returned to their guessing game.

The Arab embargo received credit for certain developments which were only remotely connected with it. Trona mining and processing had been a dynamic factor in Sweetwater County's recovery long before the energy crisis. The two large coal-fired power plants at Rock Springs and Glenrock were already expanding before the embargo. Exploration for and processing of oil, gas, and uranium were essentially continuations of high-level activity going back many years. Gas processing plants and pipelines in Campbell County were the results of discoveries in the 1960s. Unit trains had started to deliver low-sulfur coal from strip mines near Rock Springs, Hanna, and Sheridan to power plants in Iowa, Illinois, and Wisconsin in 1970, and such trains were making deliveries in seventeen states just before the Arab embargo.

The place of coal in the energy picture shifted dramatically with the jump in petroleum prices. By the mid-1970s, many saw the potential for coal as staggering in comparison with its modest past performance. By the late 1950s coal production had fallen below 2 million tons annually and then recovered only very slowly. In fact, in Wyoming's entire first century of coal mining, only about 440 million tons had been dug—small when compared with the reserves of more than 900 billion tons. Of this about 24 billion tons can be stripped in seams that vary from 11 to 200 feet thick. Much of the 96 percent which is subbituminous has low-sulfur content. This virtue means that the coal can meet sulfur emission standards in electric power generation when much eastern coal has high-sulfur content and is unacceptable.

Underground mining had produced almost all of the coal before World War II, except for the WyoDak strip mine east of Gillette in Campbell County. The gaping, black maw of the WyoDak has been a tourist attraction ever since the mine opened in 1924. Strip mining was practiced also at Hanna and Ranchester during World War II. No one objected to the early strip mines except a few underground miners who saw a threat to their jobs; and until recently no one suggested that the disturbed surface should be restored. Much of the land affected had been passed over as worthless by homesteaders before 1934. Some of the merchants and professional men in the old coal mining towns said that they preferred strip mines, explaining that they would rather have a small number of heavy equipment operators with steady work than a larger number of men working two or three days a week, as in the past, in dangerous underground mines.

Production of coal exceeded 30 million tons in 1976. Many corporations, if they had not already done so, began to look into the possibilities of converting the coal into gaseous or liquid fuels.

But ambitious hopes for coal and oil shale had to be revised. Once again a geographical limitation arose as a nemesis: lack of water. Rights to the little water that Wyoming produces had been pre-empted by downstream states in all directions because of Wyoming's later development. Wyoming was using only about one-fourth of the water it produced, and efforts to gain rights over the other three-fourths were thwarted. The greatest outflow is carried by the Snake River into Idaho. Ninety-six percent of that river's flow is committed to Idaho by a compact made in 1949 when Wyoming could not use more than 4 percent because of mountain barriers. Similarly Wyoming is limited in what it can take from the Green River to 14 percent of the flow of the Colorado River at Lee's Ferry, Arizona. By U.S. Supreme Court decree in 1945 Nebraska gets most of the North Platte River flow. Yellowstone River water cannot be exploited because of its location in a national park. Water stored in reservoirs is depleted by evaporation at the rate of four feet in one year. Part of the remainder is used by cities and towns and by rural irrigators. With so little water to begin with, and with most of it lost or pre-empted, no more than two or three coal gasification plants seem possible because in the present state of technology they require too much water. Restrictions imposed by lack of water were not taken into account in some of the early projections.

Then in 1975 when the federal government invited bids for the opportunity to develop oil shale in Colorado, Utah, and Wyoming, the three states where the largest beds in the nation lie, no bids were submitted for the Wyoming tract. The glowing promises of oil shale development had been premature. The oil unquestionably was there, but, with present technology, too much water would be required, too much air pollution would result, and disposal of the waste rock (which after processing would exceed the bulk of the original) could not be managed satisfactorily.

Also for lack of water, most of the projected coal-fired steam power plants had to be stricken from the list. The state's aridity thus eliminated many energy projects and raised serious doubts about the feasibility of others. Lack of water even stood in the way of some of the contemplated strip mines, which did not need much, but more than was readily available.

All this despite the fact that Wyoming had been the first state to claim that water belonged to the state, which it did in the constitution that Congress approved in 1890. Article VIII was one of the few original parts of that constitution, and provided for a board of control headed by a state engineer and declared that "Priority of appropriation for beneficial uses shall give the better right. No appropriation shall be denied except when such denial is demanded by the public interests." The board of control proceeded to issue water rights to irrigators on a first-come, first-served basis. Regardless of the size of the stream an appropriation is stated in terms of the right to take a definite quantity of water—so many cubic feet per second for direct flow rights, or so many acre feet for storage rights. The appropriator may use the water wherever it is needed, often far from the streambed and sometimes out of the watershed. There is no proration in time of scarcity. In a dry year, if there is only enough water in a stream for the appropriator with the oldest water right, he gets it all. A water right is private property which may be sold like land, as long as the sale does not injure other appropriators, although such transfers require the approval of the state water board. One amendment to the rights of irrigators is that municipalities now have the power to condemn rights held by irrigators.

The need for water in minerals production enhanced the market for water. When industry offered ten times as much for water as it was worth in the cattle business, some ranchers accepted. As the transfer of ranch water rights for industrial uses proceeded, with or without the land, the cow country of Wyoming was threatened. Temporarily, until the purchasers diverted the water, the irrigation continued. But a time of reckoning will come when the new owners are ready to use the water. Then less hay will be raised for winter feed, and fewer cattle will be kept through the winter. The cattle business could become one in which cattlemen in other states will send their animals to Wyoming for summer grazing only.

Faced by the urgent need for water to produce energy, the alternative to letting the ranches dry up, which no one wanted, was to develop water from sources not previously exploited. Quite a bit of Big Horn River and Green River water, allotted to Wyoming by interstate compacts, flows into other states without having been used in Wyoming because dams were never built. The enhanced value of the water in the 1970s may make it possible to put it to use. Industry may be willing to pay the cost of transferring water from the Big Horn Basin or Green River Basin to the Powder River Basin where most of the coal lies. Such a transfer would encounter opposition from residents of western Wyoming where the water will no doubt be needed a few years hence. It would cost less to transfer Big Horn River water because that stream is east of the Continental Divide and flows into the Yellowstone River. Theoretically, Wyoming should be entitled to take water out of eastern Wyoming tributaries of the Yellowstone, up to the limits of its rights in the Big Horn. However, for some not fully explained reason, a member of the Wyoming negotiating team insisted on including in the

Yellowstone River Compact (1950) a provision that water cannot be used outside of the Yellowstone Basin without approval of the other two states, Montana and North Dakota. In eastern Wyoming, the dry Gillette area is in the Cheyenne River Basin, and cannot be given Yellowstone River water without the approval of Montana and North Dakota. Montana is not likely to approve the transfer because it frowns on strip mining of coal. To get around the Yellowstone compact, Wyoming could, at great expense, pump the equivalent of its Big Horn River water uphill from Oahe Reservoir on the main stem of the Missouri River in South Dakota.

At best, development of new water will be limited and expensive. Industry prefers to buy from ranchers rather than pay more to move water from one basin to another. In a major extension of the water planning program, the legislature in 1975 authorized the State Interdepartmental Water Conference to enter the water development field. The heads of eleven state agencies concerned with water are expected to work with the director of water planning and help him in making policy.

In order to get the coal out of Wyoming and into other states, another technological marvel has been proposed: the coal slurry pipeline. Compared by some to the trans-Alaska pipeline, the coal slurry line would mix water with crushed coal in order to make it possible to pump it thousands of miles. The specific proposal involved a line to Arkansas designed to carry 25 million tons of coal a year, at a construction cost of $2 billion. The water would be obtained from deep wells in Niobrara County. The predictable enemies of such a plan—the railroads and railway unions—stalled it, as well as the refusal of Nebraska and Kansas to grant rights-of-way. Also, South Dakota threatened to sue because part of the water, if not most of it, would come from South Dakota. In 1976 it appeared unlikely that the U.S. Congress would grant eminent domain for the pipeline, although Secretary of the Interior Thomas S. Kleppe said that the Ford administration would support legislation that would give condemnation powers to slurry line builders.

Although the lack of water was the greatest inhibitor of energy development in Wyoming in the 1970s, it did not stand alone. Another obstacle was the complex land ownership pattern. Most ranches included a mixture of private, state, and federal land. The federal government owned 48 percent of the surface rights and the mineral rights under 72 percent of the land. Substantial parts of the 48 percent consisted of national forests and the two national parks, Yellowstone and Grand Teton, in which minerals development is almost unthinkable. More than three million acres of the state's sixty-two million is owned by the state, having been granted at the time of statehood, mainly to support education. It was often difficult to reconcile the several interests in a tract being considered for development. Also, the state and federal governments could not agree which of them should have superior authority in regulating the mining of federally owned minerals, although the U.S. Interior Department in 1976 agreed to let the state administer and enforce its strip mining law which was more strict than the federal law.

Capital requirements constituted a third constraint. Huge amounts of capital were needed. Industry was unwilling to risk billions in synthetic fuel projects without government subsidies. Capital, however, was less of a problem in the 1970s than ever before because many corporate giants recognized the value of the colossal coal reserves. In particular, oil companies transferred some of their recent windfall profits to coal and uranium in the belief that almost certainly they would have to take the place of oil and natural gas in the production of U.S. energy. Continental Oil, Exxon, Atlantic Richfield (Arco), Kerr-McGee, Texaco, and Standard of California (part-owner of Amax) invested heavily. Carter Oil Company (subsidiary of Exxon), Mobil, Arco, and Mapco (Mid-America Pipeline Company) each held more than 100,000 acres of state coal leases. The railroad giants, Union Pacific and Burlington Northern, had been coal producers throughout their history and owned billions of tons. They were two-way beneficiaries, from sales and from hauling. Pacific Power and Light, Idaho Power and Light, and Utah Power and Light all had substantial investments in Wyoming coal and coal-burning power plants. With such corporate giants in the vanguard it was unlikely that the "infant industry" argument could be used as effectively as it had been in the past.

The flow of billions of dollars of oil money into coal and uranium postponed fulfillment of the frequently heard prophecy that the oil men would leave Wyoming as soon as their wells ran dry. In 1976 the oil men had more money tied up in Wyoming than ever before.

The minerals lobby blocked proposals to increase taxation on coal in the 1976 legislature. Reports indicated that midwestern states which were using Wyoming coal took more revenue from the coal than Wyoming did. Yet coal did not go scot free. The 1973 legislature had raised the fossil fuels severance tax from 1 percent to 3 percent. In 1975 another 1 percent was added. Also in 1975 a special tax of .4 percent was added on coal, which was to go into an impact fund to be used for state grants to communities impacted by industrial growth. In 1976 the severance tax yielded $40 million, most of it coming from oil. Some producers could bear the burden more easily than others. Standard of Indiana, which for sixty years had been Wyoming's leading oil company, enjoyed record profits. Its net earnings (after taxes) and dividends tripled, 1966–1976.

A fourth problem, in addition to water, land, and capital, confronted developers—pressure from federal, state, and private sources to protect the environment. Concern about the environment had rarely disturbed Wyoming pioneers, except for a few sensitive souls like Bill Nye, who in 1886 wrote an essay in which he complained:

> Along the highways, where once the hopeful hundreds marched
> with long handled shovels and pick and pan . . . now the road is
> lined with empty beer bottles and peach cans. . . . You walk over
> chaos where the 'hydraulic' has plowed up the valley like a
> convulsion . . . and on all sides the rusty, neglected and humiliated
> empty tin can stares at you with its monotonous, dude-like stare.
> . . . There ain't no frontier any more. . . .[9]

When the railroads moved their tracks, as the U.P. did extensively in 1900 and 1901, they made no attempt to obliterate the original grade. The ties were left in place to rot. At Atlantic City in South Pass an ancient gold dredging operation left once

9. Edgar Wilson Nye, *Bill Nye's Remarks* (Chicago: A. E. Davis & Co., 1887), pp. 466–467.

lovely Rock Creek a shambles. Pre-1970 miners—coal, gold, copper, gravel, and bentonite—walked away from their projects without the slightest attempt to erase the scars, which people regarded as interesting records of bygone economic enterprise. Robert Sundin, director of the Wyoming Department of Environmental Quality, has directed attention to serious disturbances of land surfaces by the state highway department and private road building associated with oil drilling. Uranium exploration and mining in the 1950s and 1960s, before rehabilitation became mandatory, left countless scars and huge ugly pits in many parts of the state.

The uranium pits, totaling perhaps ten square miles, constitute the most egregious rapes of the landscape, the most shameful environmental disasters to date. Few people seem to have noticed them. The Cold War may have necessitated stockpiles of nuclear bombs but not these permanent, gaping monuments.

The chief of the regional support branch for the federal Environmental Protection Agency reported in 1973 that tailings from a uranium mill abandoned at Riverton ten years earlier were contaminating the area. Another abandoned uranium tailings pile in Converse County was identified by a federal inspector as a health hazard in April 1976. Apparently neither federal nor state agencies were prepared to do anything about the abandoned excavations and tailings piles. They were preoccupied with disputes over current and future activity.

Birds and animals have been reported poisoned by drinking water in the uranium mining areas. One University of Wyoming scientist in 1957 counted eleven dead cattle beside a ditch bulldozed to catch water pumped from exploratory holes in the Gas Hills of Fremont County. Two biologists who made a study of Shirley Basin uranium mine effluents, 1963–1966, reported that "A potentially serious pollution problem exists downstream from the study area. In time, these pollutants could seriously affect Seminoe Reservoir and the downstream portions of the North Platte River." [10]

10. Douglas L. Mitchum and Tom D. Moore, "Study of Water Pollution Problems which affect Fish and Other Aquatic Forms," p. 30. Wyoming Game and Fish Research, Laramie, 1966.

Before the adoption of federal and state clean air acts in the 1960s, most of Wyoming's air was very clean except where the people spent most of their time. In the railroad towns, smoke and cinders were accepted as inevitable. People built their homes close to the tracks, and paid no attention to the results of being downwind from locomotive smoke. Small industrial plants were allowed to locate anywhere. In Laramie a cement plant, built in 1929 just southwest of the city, needed only the prevailing southwest wind to deliver calcium oxide and cement dust to most of the homes regularly for forty years until the state's Air Quality Act (1967) forced the installation of scrubbers which abated the health hazard and nuisance.

Many townspeople had worshipped growth so long that they were reluctant to impose any restrictions on free enterprise. Gas flaring, for example, continued into the 1970s, although much less flagrantly than in the 1920s. When a few people complained about waste and smoke pollution in Campbell County's Hilight field in April 1970, Gov. Stanley K. Hathaway, chairman of the Wyoming Oil and Gas Conservation Commission, explained that the commission had limited wastage from each well to 450,000 cubic feet of gas per day. Thus, he said, the commission "tried to fulfill its responsibility to conservation and at the same time not let the momentum of development die . . . this waste is only a very small per cent of the reserves." [11] Five months later at a Casper hearing, Don Basko, Wyoming Oil and Gas Supervisor, conceded that an estimated 40 million cubic feet of gas was being flared each day. C. J. Curtis of the U.S. Geological Survey commented that in the absence of accurate measurements it might amount to 100 million instead of 40 million cubic feet. The *Casper Star-Tribune* said in an editorial, "The argument that flaring must be permitted to continue in the interest of developing the field and attracting industry is no longer valid." [12]

Although Governor Hathaway received some criticism for approving flaring, his bias in favor of the developers generally

11. *Casper Star-Tribune*, April 21, 1970.
12. *Casper Star-Tribune*, October 1, 1970.

reflected the attitude of the electorate. He was elected to a second four-year term in 1970 with 63 percent of the votes and a thirty-thousand-vote majority, greatest in the history of Wyoming gubernatorial contests. In 1976 the state supervisory board was still permitting some gas to be wasted rather than order the owner to keep the oil off the market until he could obtain a gas processing plant or pipeline transportation for both gas and oil. Some industry spokesmen blamed the waste on federal regulation of natural gas prices which left little incentive to pipeline builders.

Flush oil production and an abundance of tourists brought unprecedented prosperity for thousands of people in corporate executive positions, small business, and the professions after World War II. Many young people had more money, education, leisure, and mobility than the previous generation. Whether they left Wyoming or not, they had an enhanced appreciation of Wyoming's environmental advantages. Postwar newcomers shared in this appreciation. Even some of the old-timers began to think that growth for growth's sake was questionable, when they noticed that hunting and fishing had deteriorated under the onslaught of out-of-state tourists and sportsmen. Conscious of the skepticism about some types of growth, development-minded leaders such as Governor Hathaway began talking about "quality" growth instead of simply growth.

Persons who were becoming more concerned about the environment joined organizations such as the Wilderness Society, Audubon Society, and Izaak Walton League. The influential League of Women Voters became increasingly environment-conscious. Mike Leon of Story and Tom Bell of Lander began to ask questions about the state's future. In view of Wyoming's past history, it was to be expected that the environmentalists would not take the state by storm. Indeed, for years those who wanted drastic changes talked mainly to one another until the energy crisis attracted a few hundred recruits to their cause. Most people, however, watched from the sidelines as newcomers to the scene challenged the developers. Especially articulate were Bart Koehler and Colleen Kelly of the Wyoming Outdoor Council, Laney Hicks of the Sierra Club (Northern

Plains Office), and Lynn Dickey of the Powder River Basin
Resource Council. In 1976 each of the three organizations
claimed about 300 members. They advocated exporting Wyoming coal in preference to burning it in Wyoming; underground
mining in eastern states instead of strip mining in Wyoming;
phasing out existing strip mines; higher taxes on coal production; more study of surface reclamation; no coal-fired power
plants in Wyoming; no coal gasification, coal liquefaction, or
uranium upgrading plants; at least a two-year notice before a
major project could break ground; more careful study of impact
on water quality; protection of the traditional ranching economy;
protection of wild life; guarantee of minimum stream flow to
sustain fish and wild life, and to flush sediment and pollution;
preservation of scenic rivers; conservation of energy; land use
planning; more careful monitoring of industiral activity; no
fencing on public land; no clear cutting of timber in national
forests; in short, preservation of Wyoming, which Michael Mc-
Closkey, national executive director of the Sierra Club, described in 1973 as one of the few places in the country "left to
save." Conservative ranchers who were interested in protecting
their water joined liberal reformers in trying to maintain the
status quo. Occasionally what would have been called healthy
growth in the 1950s and early 1960s was deplored as destructive
in 1976.

The plight of two cities, Gillette and Rock Springs, drama-
tized the need for better advance planning and "front-end" financing. In the late 1960s and early 1970s oil and gas discoveries had an impact on Gillette in the northeast, and oil and gas,
trona, and construction of the Jim Bridger power plant did the
same for Rock Springs in the southwest. The two cities were in
trouble before the Arab embargo added to their problems. First
Gillette and later Rock Springs resembled the "Hell on
Wheels" boomtowns of the 1860s with their flimsy, temporary
housing; inadequate health services; sewage disposal and water
problems; high living costs; and high incidence of vice and
crime. Other communities suffered in lesser degree—Hanna,
Rawlins, Green River, Cheyenne, Casper, Douglas, Evanston,
Lyman, Buffalo, Sheridan, Wheatland, and Baggs. Gillette

grew from 3,580 in population in 1960 to an estimated 14,000 in 1976. Rock Springs grew from 11,657 in 1970 to an estimated 20,000 in 1976. Further growth was inevitable for both. Several thousand people lived in mobile homes outside of the city limits of each city. Sharon Marion, welfare worker in Rock Springs, noted the loss of a sense of community: "Impaction drowns it, kills it like that. Everybody is out for himself, for the dollar he can get and to hell with the other guy." [13] Mayor Paul Wataha of Rock Springs blamed the city's woes on the failure of industrial employers to give the city administration accurate advance information about their expansion plans. He also criticized the federal government for failure to help, the state Environmental Quality Council for directing attention to problems instead of helping alleviate them, and metropolitan newspapers for sensationalism in news stories about the city.

Pushed in some cases by the federal government, the legislature adopted a series of laws: Air Quality Act (1967), Outdoor Advertising Act (1967), Open Cut Mining Reclamation Act (1969), Land Use Act (1969), Industrial Development Information and Siting Act (1975), Environmental Quality Act (1973), Surface Mining Act (1973), and Land Use Planning Act (1975). Enforcement improved with experience and amendments.

Developers and their supporters sometimes snapped at their critics. Governor Hathaway reprehended the *High Country News* in 1973: "Mr. Bell speaks so often and it seems to me out of focus so much. He hasn't said anything good about this administration for six years." [14] The *Casper Star-Tribune* said, April 20, 1975: "Witness at present the small but strident minority—most of whom have spent scant years in Wyoming and less in actual work—clutching the hatchet, Carrie Nation fashion, and hacking away at anything that stands in their way." The *Star-Tribune,* largest paper in the state, gave the environmental organizations more space than many people thought they deserved. For various reasons awareness of environmental problems increased. The Wyoming Outdoor Council, which rated

13. *Wyoming Eagle* (Cheyenne), May 28, 1976.
14. *Casper Star-Tribune,* February 9, 1973.

the ninety-two members of the legislature on environmental issues, gave forty members 70 percent or better in 1975–1976 compared to only sixteen members in 1973–1974.

The power of the energy companies, if they worked in concert, was so overwhelming that only the federal government had much chance to block them. Fortunately, the corporation executives in general were more enlightened and responsible than had been the case before the Great Depression. The Union Pacific, in particular, resembled not at all the predepression corporation from which it had evolved.

In line with the traditional kowtowing to industry lobbyists, most legislators in the 1970s still paid more attention to them than to the environmentalists. So did their constituents. Three political scientists at the University of Wyoming, who conducted a statewide survey in the fall of 1974, found that the citizens had favorable images of the oil and coal industries. Only 8.8 percent responded negatively; 76.6 percent indicated "slightly good" to "extremely good" attitudes. Another survey in 1976 revealed that 79 percent of the residents of Campbell County, one of two areas receiving greatest impact, approved of industrial development. Yet 60 percent of the Campbell County respondents conceded that they did not like the rapid population growth.

When President Gerald Ford nominated Stanley K. Hathaway to be secretary of the interior in 1975, just after he had retired from his two four-year terms as governor, environmentalists opposed his confirmation on the grounds that he was too industry-oriented and had promoted strip mining and coal-burning power plants. The most comprehensive analysis of Hathaway's environmental record was the one prepared by the staff of the Environmental Defense Fund's Denver office for presentation in the U.S. Senate hearings. The most effective hostile critics in the hearings were Bart Koehler of the Wyoming Outdoor Council and four members of the Senate Committee—Floyd K. Haskell of Colorado, James Abourezk of South Dakota, Richard Stone of Florida, and John Glenn of Ohio.

The extended hearings before the Senate Committee on Interior and Insular Affairs established that Governor Hathaway had led the drive for growth in his first term, 1967–1971, that his efforts were supported by most of his constituents, and that, like his constituents, he had slowly modified his attitude toward growth and had accepted some restraints to protect the environment during his second term, 1971–1975.

No Wyoming citizen had ever served in the president's cabinet. Hathaway's nomination was endorsed enthusiastically by leaders of both political parties, newspaper editors, and people all over the state. Hathaway had been one of the most popular governors in the state's history and the only one who had served more than six years.

Although Hathaway won Senate confirmation, 60–36, after much sharp questioning, he resigned six weeks later and returned to Cheyenne to practice law. He received a hero's welcome in Wyoming. His decision to resign resulted from a combination of factors, among them, exhaustion from the ordeal of the hearings, subsequent overwork as he tried to master the complexities of the Interior Department in a few weeks, his failure to get his nominee as undersecretary approved, the realization that the environmentalists in the department would try to thwart his every decision with respect to energy development, and brief hospitalization for what was diagnosed as depression and a mild case of diabetes.

Meanwhile the Sierra Club delayed some of the strip mining on federal land in the Powder River Basin about a year and a half in 1975–1976. The National Environmental Policy Act passed by Congress in 1969 had provided that all agencies of the federal government must prepare impact statements before major federal actions "significantly affecting the quality of the human environment." The Sierra Club, Northern Plains Office, in association with four other groups (National Wildlife Federation, League of Women Voters of Montana and South Dakota, Montana Wilderness Association, and Northern Plains Resource Council) had filed a lawsuit in federal district court to require the Department of the Interior to issue a regional environmental impact statement for the entire Fort Union Coal formation, which extends from the Powder River Basin of Wyoming into Montana, North Dakota, and South Dakota. The case was taken to the court of appeals, Washington, D.C., which issued an injunction, January 3, 1975, against any new mining or railroad development on federal land in the four-state area. Mining on private land, state land, or on federal land was not affected; so mining continued but not at the pace anticipated.

After a few mining plans and housing projects had been shelved and a few hundred workers laid off, the *Casper Star-Tribune* exploded, December 20, 1975:

> . . . the people of Wyoming and the U.S., and that includes working people and business, are sick to death of do gooders seeking a role in life. They are not producers but living off the sweat of others and the donations they beg off well meaning individuals.
>
> It is also typical of this group that they crank up their press releases from bosky beauty spots in Wyoming—Jackson Hole, Dubois, Story. When is the last time you heard from them from the mining country like Hanna, Rock Springs, Gillette? When is the last time they talked to working people there struggling to make homes for their families? That's hardly their style.

In a setback for the plaintiffs, the U.S. Supreme Court in January 1976 accepted an appeal of the case and lifted the appeals court injunction which had forbidden all new activity on federal land. The Burlington Northern and Chicago and North Western railroads immediately began building a 126-mile railroad from Douglas to Gillette to expedite coal export.

Before the Supreme Court, Wyoming's attorney general, Frank Mendicino, and others argued that the regional impact statement sought by the plaintiffs should be required. The Interior Department lawyers, on the other hand, argued that the department's six-volume impact statement for the eastern part of the Powder River Basin and additional localized studies for specific mines ought to suffice. They maintained that there had been no proposal for regional action, only private applications for leases, and that the granting of one lease did not require the government to grant another. The Supreme Court in a unanimous decision on June 28, 1976, ruled in favor of the Interior Department, making the broad impact statement unnecessary.

Other impact statements, required by both federal and state

governments, would continue to keep many people busy. These statements are many-faceted. For instance, a 300-page statement published in 1975 by the U.S. Geological Survey for the Cordero mine twenty miles southeast of Gillette covers the impact of the mining operation on climate, air quality, topography, soils, mineral resources, water resources, vegetation, wildlife, fish, recreation, agriculture, transportation, aesthetics, socioeconomic conditions, and archaeological, paleontological, and historical values. The public was invited to read copies which were placed in convenient libraries and to file written comments within forty-five days. "Environmental impact statements—do they do any Good?" asked Dr. Harold L. Bergman, assistant professor of zoology and physiology, University of Wyoming, in the June 1976 issue of *Wyoming Wildlife*. Dr. Bergman answered "yes," and explained that the impact statements do tend to eliminate federal boondoggle projects; give incentive to planners to think early and carefully about potential impact problems; open details of projects to the public and invite comments; and make federal and state agencies vulnerable to lawsuits if statutory procedural requirements are not met.

Professors of range management and other specialists at the University of Wyoming, after years of experimentation, tended to agree that the land in the Powder River Basin—mostly semi-arid, gently rolling, shortgrass land—could be revegetated and made more productive than it had been before it was strip mined, but not with the same native plants. The soil removed would have to be stockpiled and returned. Irrigation might be necessary for several years until the plants could take hold. Hummocks and gullies, which in the past have been valuable for protecting cattle in winter, could not be replaced. On the other hand, in some places the range might be improved by only partially filling excavations and converting them into stock ponds. A thorough renovation job might cost as much as $3,000 an acre in some parts of the Powder River Basin.

When the Sierra Club injunction was lifted in 1976, the Interior Department terminated a moratorium on federal leases which it had declared in 1971. Secretary of the Interior Thomas Kleppe, however, announced that the department did not expect any coal leasing for a year or more, inasmuch as quite a few leases issued in 1970 and before had not yet been developed. In the meantime the department would prepare ten regional environmental impact statements, refine the competitive leasing process, and accept applications for new leases.

Wyoming's expansion of strip mining was moving ahead in 1976 with more deliberation than had been expected in 1974. Production of about 30 million tons of coal in 1976 was less than double the output of 1973. Yet the pace of change would soon accelerate. Whereas only two coal mines were operating in Campbell County in August 1976, twelve others were in various stages of planning or construction, and sixty applications for new federal leases had recently been filed. At the rate coal companies were signing contracts with electric utilities as far away as Indiana and Texas, it was not too much to expect production of 100 million tons in 1980 and 200 million tons a few years later.

Since the U.S. Bureau of Reclamation can supply no more than about 200 megawatts (200 million watts) of power from hydroelectric plants, Wyoming has to depend mainly on coal for its electricity. During the three years following the Arab embargo, expansion planned or already under way occurred at the three large coal-fired steam generating plants—Rock Springs, Glenrock, and Kemmerer—and an enlargement of an experimental plant at Gillette. Ordinarily between one-half and two-thirds of the power from the coal-fired plants is exported to other states.

The only major new industrial plant started during 1973–1976 was the Missouri Basin Power Project's Laramie River Station near Wheatland, where construction began in July 1976. The plant is scheduled to have three 500-megawatt units, the first of which is to be operational in 1980. The plant will serve a large number of consumer-owned utilities in eight states. Environmentalists tried for two or three years to block the project. The builders, however, won the support of most of the Wheatland residents and that of state agencies by offering financial assistance to relieve part of the impact, by constructing both temporary and permanent housing in advance of need, and by promising to have no more than 2,250 workers on the project at any one time.

A new threat to the Wheatland plant appeared in December 1976. The state of Nebraska filed a suit alleging that the plant would use water rightfully belonging to Nebraska.

In 1976, as in every election year, many Wyoming residents denounced the federal government. Although Republican candidates for office did most of the denouncing, Democrats participated occasionally. There were too many federal agencies to deal with, too much delay, too much paperwork, and too much double-talk, it was alleged. For a century Wyoming's relations with federal agencies had been strained much of the time. Since the 1870s most of the conflict had centered around control and use of federal lands. In New Deal days the proliferation of federal agencies and the large number of federal employees ("bureaucrats") became a major grievance. A Worland lawyer wrote to U.S. Sen. Joseph C. O'Mahoney in May 1937 that "People are feeling the same way as the framers of the Declaration of Independence felt when they wrote: 'He has erected a multitude of new offices, and sent hither swarms of officers to harass our people, and eat out their substance.' " [15]

In the 1970s a flood of complex regulations and excessive paperwork caused the greatest distress. In 1976 President William Carlson of the University of Wyoming complained to a legislative committee that it would cost the university millions of dollars to comply with regulations established by federal agencies without congressional approval. Especially irritating was the fact that federal employees received better pay and retirement benefits than state and local government employees.

The federal government regularly spends more money in Wyoming than it takes out in taxes. In 1975, for example, Wyoming received $1.21 for each tax dollar it sent to Washington. [16] U.S. Sen. Gale W. McGee, who had been responsible for bringing more federal money to Wyoming than any of his pre-

15. O'Mahoney MSS, University of Wyoming Library, file drawer 37, file folder "Supreme Court Reorganization Plan—1937." Used with permission.

16. *National Journal,* June 26, 1976, pp. 878–891.

decessors in the Senate, said in 1976: "It's time we stop bad-mouthing the government of the United States . . . we have the finest government in the world." [17] Senator McGee, who was seeking election to a fourth term but lost, pointed out that the "Federal Connection" had brought many benefits to the state at the request of its citizens. He urged confidence in the federal system and constructive criticism "based on cold, hard fact." McGee's successful opponent was a wealthy cattleman, Malcolm Wallop, who promised to reduce drastically the federal bureaucracy and to return government to the people. Wallop received 55 percent of the vote, Gerald Ford, 60 percent.

The most important questions facing Wyoming residents in 1976 were what industrial plants and how many people would come to the state in the near future. The U.S. Bureau of the Census had estimated the state's population to be 374,000 in 1975, which was 41,584 more than that of 1970. Congressman Teno Roncalio guessed that the state would have 500,000 people in 1985. Gov. Ed Herschler's guess for 1985 was 750,000. The thought that a state which had required more than a century to accumulate 375,000 people might have to absorb another 375,000 in a single decade caused much uneasiness from border to border.

17. *Laramie Daily Boomerang,* June 15, 1976.

Epilogue

$\mathcal{T}$HE role of Wyoming in the first two centuries of the United States has been to play almost no role. Or at least, to have taken only a minor part in the sweeping developments that overtook the rest of the country. Wyoming was the place passed by, the high country with a trendy fur product that a few hundred people paid attention to when the getting was good but a place allowed to recede afterward into its silent snows and granite ridges of isolation. The Platte River Road could carry hundreds of thousands through Wyoming and then leave behind only its ruts for later inhabitants to ponder. Wyoming could peek at the world during the romantic days of the cowboy but then fade back behind the fences of its spiritual corral, nursing a fond image of the Old West while outside forces turned the ranch into an economic unit. And now that Wyoming has become the cynosure of energy producers, it is torn between the allure of development and the price it fears must be exacted for that development.

But in between and during all these happenings, a few people came to live in Wyoming, liked it, and stayed. As a rule they were remarkably realistic people, understanding exactly why others would not want to live in such a land. But they were also slightly sentimental about the place, its climate, its hidden surprises. One of them, a student at the University of Wyoming in 1975, wrote this about Buffalo, population 3,354, near the Big Horn Mountains:

There are still a few around with characteristics of the "old west"—the tough, tobacco-chewin', cussin', hard drinkin', have-a-good-fight-on-Saturday-night gang—whom I don't particularly enjoy, but there are many decent people. Buffalo is also pretty exclusive about accepting newcomers to the community, but again, they are very hospitable to tourists and helpful to people who get in a jam. It could be described as a boisterous community, dominated by large cattle ranchers and Basque sheepherders, whose favorite pastime seems to be drinking and telling tall tales.

Just the sort of place a suburbanite might want to pass through in a Winnebago, but not linger in, or the place a city dweller might visit to reinforce his prejudices about the West. But definitely not for lengthy stays, because it's a long way to the nearest professional football stadium or beach, and the cultural fare is definitely limited.

Not that Wyoming doesn't see the speck that is in its own eye. Another university student wrote of a home town:

> Powell is a very sheltered community which is good in some ways yet bad in others. Not one Negro family lives in the town though three or four Negroes play basketball for the college every year. Each summer Mexican beet laborers come and work the beets, and some Mexican families live there the year round. These permanent residents seem to fit in very well, though the transients occasionally exhibit hostile behavior.[1]

And another kind of resident appeared in Wyoming during this century: the cosmopolitan urbanite sick of the dirt and turmoil and fast pace of the big city, escaping to peace and solitude and the rigors of outdoor life. For these people the appeal of Wyoming lies precisely in its rejection by everyone else. Writer Otis Carney, one such dropout from the rat race, bought a ranch in Wyoming in the 1960s, locating near Cora, on the upper reaches of the Green and just west of the Wind River Mountains. During several years of ranching, he, his wife, and their three sons discovered what oldtimers have always known: ranching may be fun to read about but takes muscle, grit, and endurance just to make a bare minimum of profit. In this time

---

1. Both quotations from students are used with permission.

the Carneys could learn what it means to be frozen in by high drifts of snow, to witness newborn calves still steaming in the cold dews of early spring, to sweat under the sun while stacking huge mountains of hay, to stand in awe as swans ascend from a marsh against an orange-gray autumn sky. Carney, who kept on writing even while working his ranch, finally concluded life for a family on a Wyoming ranch meant something:

> You can't be very smart to spend your life and dreams on two of the oldest, most underpaid professions in the world: the pasturing of beasts and the telling of tales . . . .
> Yes, but what was pay compared to those times? . . . How many men had their wives and family beside them, as I'd had? A common struggle, never quite winning; but doing was all that mattered.
> Chasing a dream, and realizing *that,* right there, was the whole ball game.[2]

Wyoming still has its dreams, not only of the past, but of the future, and these hopes and visions are now threatened by forces not always under the control of the people of Wyoming.

For those who had no neighbors will now see many new faces.

And the land no one wanted for centuries is now coveted by hosts of outsiders.

The country where the wind blew in primeval purity will now breathe new odors and smokes.

Almost no part of the country has the opportunity now facing Wyoming: to demonstrate what America could have been if planners and developers had traded some short-term profits for long-term gains. It is possible that Wyoming could emerge from its primitive isolation but in such a way that its greatest values are preserved and its old way of life left for those who choose to follow it.

Development does not necessarily have to be a story of un-mitigated, unrelieved disaster. While it appears that the people of Wyoming are going to have to sacrifice in part some of the

2. Otis Carney, *New Lease on Life: The Story of a City Family Who Quit the Rat Race and Moved to a Ranch in Wyoming* (New York: Random House, 1971), pp. 169–170.

things they have valued most, there is still hope that much can be salvaged. The doubling of population by 1985 may not, after all, occur. Congressman Teno Roncalio, whose credentials as a forecaster are quite as good as Governor Herschler's, has predicted that the population in 1985 will be not 750,000 but only 500,000. The smaller, more manageable number is plausible. Five thousand men with modern equipment can strip mine 200 million tons of coal in a year. The families, storekeepers, entertainers, and so on could not number more than 40,000. And Wyoming's coal output may not exceed 200 million tons in 1985. Lack of water will rule out most of the labor-intensive projects that have been proposed, although a few more power plants and two coal gasification plants are likely.

If the population does not exceed 500,000 in 1985, it should be possible to save enough of the traditional lifestyle to keep most of the natives and many of the immigrants happy. It should be possible to sustain the livestock industry and crop agriculture at close to their present level. Tourism may even expand without too much loss of quality. The state's several national forests, state parks, and many lakes and reservoirs can absorb more tourists than visit them now. Maintaining quality hunting and fishing will tax the ingenuity of the Game and Fish Department, but its experts may find ways to do it. The state's two most popular tourist attractions, Yellowstone and Grand Teton national parks, are already crowded, leading to suggestions that new roads might be built to open areas of Yellowstone where hitherto tourists have not gone. This would be disastrous to wildlife and generally would do more harm than good. Whatever happens, the state's two most spectacular scenic attractions must be protected against abuse. For pure, overwhelming beauty they excel anything else of their kind in the United States. One is the Teton Mountains viewed from across Jackson Lake or Jenny Lake. The other is the lower falls of the Yellowstone River, with the river and the Grand Canyon of the Yellowstone in the foreground, viewed from Artist's Point.

In 1887 Owen Wister camped out in the Wind River Mountains and one night by the light of a flickering fire wrote to his mother:

The weather has been so lovely that we have slept beneath the stars without even a tent over our heads. The river we follow farther and farther into the mountains is possessed with every magic a river has had allotted to it. Clear green to the bottom—rushing and tumbling—cool to go into, cast over, and full of trout that live behind the jutting rocks under wild rose bushes. Each night we camp by it, and when we leave it I shall go into mourning.[3]

Perhaps it is not yet time to grieve; Wyoming still has enough of the old magic to stir the blood of visitor and native alike. But surely it is time to reflect on the joy that Wister savored, and ponder whether what the world wants from Wyoming is worth more than what Wyoming already offers the world.

3. Owen Wister, *Owen Wister Out West: His Journals and Letters,* ed. Fanny Kemble Wister (Chicago: University of Chicago Press), pp. 50–51.

Suggestions for Further Reading

The energy crisis has put pressure on anthropologists and archaeologists to study early man sites before they will be destroyed by coal strip mining. Valuable background studies are Hannah Marie Wormington, *Ancient Man in North America* (Denver: Denver Museum of Natural History, 1957); William T. Mulloy, *A Preliminary Historical Outline for the Northwestern Plains* (Laramie: University of Wyoming, 1958); Mulloy, *Archaeological Investigations along the North Platte River in Eastern Wyoming* (Laramie: University of Wyoming, 1965); George C. Frison, ed., *The Casper Site, A Hell Gap Bison Kill on the High Plains* (New York: Academic Press, 1974); and Url Lanham, *The Bone Hunters* (New York: Columbia University Press, 1973). Lanham discusses the activities of paleontologists during the years 1850–1900.

Studies of native Americans which merit special attention are Harold P. Howard, *Sacajawea* (Norman: University of Oklahoma Press, 1971); Irving Anderson, "Probing the Riddle of the Bird Woman," *Montana the magazine of Western History,* 23 (October 1973):2–17; Grace Raymond Hebard, *Washakie* (Cleveland: A. H. Clark, 1930); Mae Urbanek, *Chief Washakie of the Shoshones* (Boulder: Johnson Publishing Co., 1971); Virginia Cole Trenholm and Maurine Carley, *The Shoshonis, Sentinels of the Rockies* (Norman: University of Oklahoma Press, 1965); Trenholm, *The Arapahoes, Our People* (Norman: University of Oklahoma Press, 1970); James C. Olson, *Red Cloud and the Sioux Problem* (Lincoln: University of Nebraska Press, 1965); and Tom Shakespeare, *The Sky People* (New York: The Vantage Press, 1971).

Fur trade history is well told in these books: Don Berry, *A Majority of Scoundrels, An Informal History of the Rocky Mountain Fur Company* (New York: Harper, 1961); Bernard De Voto, *Across the Wide Missouri* (Boston: Houghton Mifflin, 1947); Washington Irving, *Astoria* (Norman: University of Oklahoma Press, 1964); David Lavender, *The Fist in the Wilderness* (Garden City, N.Y.: Doubleday, 1964); Dale L. Morgan, *Jedediah Smith and the Opening of the West* (Indianapolis: Bobbs-Merrill, 1953); Dale L. Morgan, *The West of William H. Ashley* (Denver: Old West Publishing Company, 1964); David Muench, *Rendezvous Country* (Palo Alto: American West Publishing Company, 1975); Walter O'Meara, *Daughters of the Country, the Women of the Fur Traders and Mountain Men* (New York: Harcourt, Brace & World, 1968); Osborne Russell, *Journal of a Trapper* (Lincoln: University of Nebraska Press, 1965); and Lewis O. Saum, *The Fur Trader and the Indian* (Seattle: University of Washington Press, 1965).

The following works offer excellent reading about the overland trails: David Lavender, *Westward Vision, the Story of the Oregon Trail* (New York: McGraw-Hill, 1963, paperback, 1971); Dale L. Morgan, *Overland in 1846, Diaries and Letters of the California-Oregon Trail* (Georgetown, Calif.: Talisman Press, 1963); Dale L. Morgan, ed., *The Overland Diary of James A. Pritchard from Kentucky to California in 1849* (Denver: The Old West Publishing Company, 1969); Robert L. Munkres, *Saleratus and Sagebrush: the Oregon Trail through Wyoming* (Cheyenne: State Archives and Historical Department, 1974); Walter Stegner, *The Gathering of Zion, The Story of the Mormon Trail* (New York: McGraw-Hill, 1964); and George R. Stewart, *The California Trail* (New York: McGraw-Hill, 1962).

Robert A. Murray deals knowledgeably with one of his favorite subjects in *Military Posts in the Powder River Country of Wyoming 1865–1894* (Lincoln: University of Nebraska Press, 1968) and *Military Posts of Wyoming* (Fort Collins: Old Army Press, 1974). The standard work on Wyoming's most famous fort is still LeRoy R. Hafen and F. M. Young, *Fort Laramie and the Pageant of the West, 1834–1890* (Glendale, Calif.: A. H. Clark, 1938). Fort Bridger's history is covered in J. Cecil Alter, *James Bridger,* issued at various times by three different publishers, and Fred R. Gowans and Eugene E. Campbell, *Fort Bridger: Island in the Wilderness* (Provo: Brigham Young University Press, 1975).

The Wyoming Country Before Statehood, by L. Milton Woods (Worland, Wyo.: Worland Press, 1971) is a thorough study, with excellent maps, of the Spanish, French, Mexican, British, and Texas claims to the Wyoming country and of the many U.S. territories which had jurisdiction over the area before 1868.

William H. Goetzmann has written two important books that are described in their titles: *Army Exploration in the American West, 1803–1863* (New Haven: Yale University Press, 1959) and *Exploration and Empire: the explorer and the scientist in the winning of the American West* (New York: Knopf, 1966).

Among recent excellent books on a popular subject are H. Duane Hampton, *How the U.S. Cavalry Saved Our National Parks* (Bloomington: Indiana University Press, 1971); Aubrey Haines, *Yellowstone National Park, Its Exploration and Establishment* (Washington, D.C.: U.S. Department of the Interior, National Park Service, 1974); and Richard A. Bartlett, *Nature's Yellowstone* (Albuquerque: University of New Mexico Press, 1974). Grand Teton National Park, which lies just south of Yellowstone, has found able interpreters in David J. Saylor, who wrote *Jackson Hole, Wyoming: in the Shadows of the Tetons* (Norman: University of Oklahoma Press, 1971), and Frank J. Calkins, whose work is entitled *Jackson Hole* (New York: Alfred A. Knopf, 1973).

The Union Pacific Railroad has inspired scores of books. Two of the best are Barry B. Combs, *Westward to Promontory; Building the Union Pacific across the Plains and Mountains* (Palo Alto: American West Publishing Company, 1969) and Robert G. Athearn, *Union Pacific Country* (New York: Rand-McNally, 1971).

The lore of cattlemen and cowboys has occupied thousands of authors. Among the better books about the Wyoming cattle industry are John Clay, *My Life on the Range* (Norman: University of Oklahoma Press, 1962—originally privately printed in Chicago in 1924); Ernest S. Osgood, *The Day of the Cattleman* (Minneapolis: University of Minnesota Press, 1929 and 1954, and later by the University of Chicago Press); Louis Pelzer, *The Cattlemen's Frontier* (Glendale, Calif.: A. H. Clark, 1936); Maurice Frink, W. T. Jackson, and A. W. Spring, *When Grass Was King* (Boulder: University of Colorado Press, 1956); Maurice Frink, *Cow Country Cavalcade* (Denver: Old West Publishing Co., 1954); Robert H. Burns, A. S. Gillespie, and W. G. Richardson, *Wyoming's Pioneer Ranches* (Laramie: Top-of-the-World Press, 1955); Helena Huntington Smith, *The War on Powder River* (New

York: McGraw-Hill, 1966); Gene M. Gressley, *Bankers and Cattlemen* (New York: Alfred A. Knopf, 1966—and in paperback, University of Nebraska Press, 1971); and John Rolfe Burroughs, *Guardian of the Grasslands, The First Hundred Years of the Wyoming Stock Growers Association* (Cheyenne: Pioneer Printing Co., 1971).

The wool industry has attracted few authors. Edward N. Wentworth wrote the classic account in *America's Sheep Trails: history, personalities* (Ames: Iowa State College Press, 1948).

Ted Olson describes with sensitivity his recollections of growing up on a Wyoming ranch in *Ranch on the Laramie* (Boston: Little, Brown and Co., 1973).

Exemplary books by women homesteaders are: Elinore Pruitt Stewart, *Letters of a Woman Homesteader* (Boston: Houghton Mifflin, 1913—also in paperback—Lincoln: University of Nebraska Press, 1961); Florence Blake Smith, *Cow Chips 'n' Cactus* (New York: Pageant Press, 1962); and Bessie Lee Rehwinkel, *Dr. Bessie* (St. Louis: Concordia Publishing House, 1963).

The best account of the early history of the rodeo business is Clifford P. Westermeier's *Man, Beast, Dust* (Denver: World Press, 1947).

Wyoming's most famous humorist, Bill Nye, wrote fourteen books under twenty titles in the 1880s and 1890s. The best introduction to Nye and his humor may be found in a book by one of Nye's sons, Frank Wilson Nye, entitled *Bill Nye, his own Life Story* (New York: Century Co., 1926). A gathering of Nye's humor has been edited by T. A. Larson in *Bill Nye's Western Humor* (Lincoln: University of Nebraska Press, 1968).

T. A. Larson's *History of Wyoming* (Lincoln: University of Nebraska Press, 1965) will be brought up to date in a revised edition by the same press.

Among other books worth reading are Don Russell, *The Lives and Legends of Buffalo Bill* (Norman: University of Oklahoma Press, 1960); Lewis L. Gould, *Wyoming: A Political History, 1868–1896* (New Haven: Yale University Press, 1968); David J. Wasden, *From Beaver to Oil: A Century in the Development of Wyoming's Big Horn Basin* (Cheyenne: Pioneer Printing & Stationery Co., 1973); John F. Reiger, *American Sportsmen and the Origins of Conservation* (New York: Winchester Press, 1975); and Bill Bragg, *Wyoming's Wealth; A History of Wyoming* (Basin, Wyo.: Big Horn Publishers, 1976).

The *Wyoming Historical Blue Book: A Legal and Political History of Wyoming 1868–1943* (Denver: Bradford-Robinson Printing Co., 1946) is an invaluable reference work, which was compiled by Marie H. Erwin originally, and was brought up to date and published in three volumes with the title *Wyoming Blue Book* (Cheyenne: Wyoming State Archives and Historical Department, 1974).

One who prefers to absorb his history through fiction can do no better than to read A. B. Guthrie, *The Big Sky* (Boston: Houghton Mifflin, 1947) and *The Way West* (New York: William Sloane Associates, 1949); Robert A. Roripaugh, *Honor Thy Father* (New York: William Morrow, 1963); Peggy Simson Curry, *The Oil Patch* (New York: McGraw-Hill, 1959); and James A. Michener, *Centennial* (New York: Random House, 1974, and Fawcett Crest Book, 1975).

Two modern bibliographies which will be useful to anyone who wishes to go beyond the necessarily limited reading list offered here are Mae and Jerry Urbanek's *Know Wyoming, a guide to its literature* (Boulder: Johnson Publishing Co., 1969), and "A Selective Literary Bibliography of Wyoming," by Richard F. Fleck and Robert A. Campbell in *Annals of Wyoming* 46 (Spring 1974): 75–112. Fleck and Campbell added a one-page supplement to their bibliography in the *Annals of Wyoming* 47 (Fall 1975): 234. Readers are reminded that the *Annals of Wyoming,* official publication of the Wyoming State Historical Society, contains many articles and book reviews. It is published biannually (spring and fall) by the State Archives and Historical Department, Cheyenne. This important journal began publication in 1925.

Index

American Fur Company: headed by John Jacob Astor, 17; and the Shoshonis, 19; sent brigade into the Green River Valley, 32–33; competition with Rocky Mountain Fur Company, 33; agreement with Bill Sublette, 34–35; bought Fort Laramie, 35; discontinued rendezvous, 36–37; taken over by U.S. Army, 51. *See also* Fur trade; Astor, John Jacob

Anthony, Susan B., 81, 82, 83, 97

Arapaho Indians: competed for best hunting grounds, 5; killed Jacques LaRamie, 21; in the nineteenth century, 64–67; killed by Connor's army, 68; 1868 treaty, 73–74

Arikara Indians, 13, 23, 28

Ashley, Gen. William H. (congressman): advertisement for 100 "Enterprising Young Men," 22; ambition, 22; Ashley-Henry partnership, 22–23; and the Green River Valley, 24–27; and the rendezvous, 26–27; successful fur trader, 27; proposed the name Wyoming, 72–73; opposed territorial organization, 75

Astor, John Jacob, 17, 19, 21

Astoria, 17, 19

Averell, James, 129

Baker, Jim, 38

Baker, Nathan A., 114, 115

Bates, Capt. A. E., 74

Beadle, J. H., 97

Beaver. *See* Fur trade

Bell, Tom, 171, 173

Bergman, Dr. Harold L., 177

Bison. *See* Buffalo

"Black 14" incident, 105–106

Blackfeet Indians, 16, 17, 23, 33

Bonneville, Capt. B. L. E., 33–34, 149

Bozeman Trail, 68, 69, 73–74

Bridger, James (Jim): and Hugh Glass, 23; in first rank among mountain men, 24, 36, 55; visited Yellowstone Park, 29; and the Rocky Mountain Fur Company, 31–32; bought Fort Laramie, 35; taught Jim Baker, 38; trading post proprietor, 55–56; and Louis Vasquez, 55–60 *passim;* fame as a guide, 56; terminated trading activities, 57–58; met Brigham Young, 58; sold his fort, 60, 61; blacksmith's apprentice, 63; warned of Indian trouble, 63

Bright, William H. ("Colonel"), 77–80, 84–85, 92

Brock, J. Elmer, 157

Brown, M. C., 145

Buffalo: *Bison antiquus*, 3; did not thrive, 5; robe trade, 35, 57; herds on the range-land, 109, 113

Buffalo (town), 181–182

Burdette, S. S., 118

Burton, Sir Richard, 52, 53

Campbell, John A. (governor): immigration commission, 78; and woman suffrage, 80–81, 88, 89, 93; bribe offer, 88; president of the Wyoming Stock and Wool Growers Association, 114, 115; replaced by Thayer, 117

Campbell, Robert, 34–35

Carey, Joseph M. (governor): delegate to Congress, 95, 100; and the cowboy, 122; and cattlemen, 127; workmen's compensation act, 148–149; nonpolitical tax commission, 158

Carlson, William, 179

Carney, Otis, 182–183

Carrington, Col. Henry B., 68–69

Carrington, Margaret I., 53–54

192

Nye, William (Bill): comments on climate, 5–6; described the cowboys, 121–122; and dry-farming, 135; essay on the environment, 168

Oil industry: raw material until the 1890s, 149–150; profit during World War I, 150; Ohio Oil Company (Marathon), 150, 151; refinery in Casper, 150, 152; Standard of Indiana, 150, 151, 152, 168; the roustabout, 151; capital intensive, 151–152; Teapot Dome, 152–153; taxation, 153–159; production, 155, 160, 161; gasoline prices, 156; conservation inaction, 156–157; price tripled, 161; energy crisis, 161–163; shale development, 163, 164; capital requirements, 167–168

O'Mahoney, Joseph C., 103, 141, 179

Oregon Trail: and the Astorians, 19, 21; other names, 40, 44; monotonous travel, 46; emigrants in 1841, 49. *See also* Platte River Road

Pacific Fur Company, 17, 19

Palmer, Joel, 57

Parker, Samuel, 40

Pershing, John J., 141

Petroleum. *See* Oil industry

Phillips, John "Portugee," 68–69

Pike, Lt. Zebulon M., 42–43

Pinedale, 38, 161

Platte River Road; left its ruts, 40, 181; highway, 44–45; failure of towns and cities to develop, 50–51; patrolled, 62; great migration, 63–65; as dangerous, 67; odd assortment of settlers, 70. *See also* Oregon Trail

Politics and government: several governments claiming ownership, 5; territory, 70–73, 90; laws and rights of women, 81–82; "first woman judge," 84–85, 91; women on juries, 85–87; secret ballot, 87–88; ratio of voting-age men to women in 1890, 96; 1889 constitutional convention, 98–100, 105, 128, 145; statehood, 99–100, 136; more Democrats than Republicans, 100; first state to elect a woman to state office, 102; woman governor, 102–103; initiative and referendum amendment, 105; state's posture with respect to reform, 106; Dingley Tariff, 131–132; stockmen in, 140–141; workmen's compensation act, 148–149; welfare recipients, 157; laws affecting the environment, 173; power of the energy companies, 174; federal government expenditures in Wyoming, 179–180. *See also* Homestead Act; Livestock; Suffrage; Women; World War I; World War II

Pony Express, 45–46

Population: smallness of in Wyoming, 3, 7, 50, 110, 143; first known human beings in area, 3–4; depopulated for 2,000 years, 4; first trickle of immigrants, 40–41; during migration period, 50; "service industry," 51; immigration commission, 78; foreign-born in 1870, 82; preponderance of males, 90–91, 104; in 1869, 108; rise in number of settlers in 1920s, 135–136; in 1975, 180; for 1985, 180, 184

—censuses: of 1870, 89–90; of 1890, 100, 102; of 1970, 143, 160, 180

—emigrants: traffic between 1841 and 1868, 44–46; "seeing the elephant," 48; guides for, 49–50; trading posts, 51–52, 63; and ferries, 60–62; and bridges, 61–62; need for draft animals, 62; blacksmiths, 62–63; as short of cash, 63; on the Platte River Road, 63–65; as contributors to creation of Wyoming Territory, 70–71

Post, Mrs. Morton E. (Amalia), 81, 92–93, 98

Potts, Daniel, 29

Potts, John, 15

Powder River, 13, 14, 68

Powder River Basin, 175–177

Powell, John Wesley, 69, 118, 128

Powell (town), 182

Railroads: Pacific Railway Acts of 1862 and 1864, 70–71; focused national attention on Wyoming, 71–72, 74–75; failure to bring settlers, 78; Chinese employees of, 90, 146–147, first transcontinental, 108; Union Pacific, 144, 146; and taxes, 146; "Rock Springs Massacre,"

_ RO — MAN

CX0071265001